Letts

Framework FOCUS

Speaking and Listening

Cathi Allison

Published by Letts Educational
The Chiswick Centre
414 Chiswick High Road
London W4 5TF

t 020 89963333
f 020 87428390
e mail@lettsed.co.uk
w www.letts-education.com

Letts Educational Limited is a division of Granada Learning Limited, part of the Granada Media Group.

First published 2002

ISBN 1840857064

British Library Cataloguing in Publication Data
A catalogue record for this book is available from the British Library.

Acknowledgements
The publishers would like to thank the following for permission to use copyright material. Every effort has been made to trace copyright holders and to obtain their permission for the use of copyright material. The author and publishers will gladly receive information enabling them to rectify any error or omission in subsequent editions.

Developed and packaged by McLean Press Ltd

Commissioned by Helen Clark

Project management by Vicky Butt

Edited by Gavin McLean

Cover design by bigtop, Bicester, UK

Internal design by bigtop, Bicester, UK

Illustrations by James Arnold, Linda Combi, Nick Duffy, Tony Forbes, Nigel Kitching.

Production by PDQ

Printed and bound in the UK by Ashford Colour Press

Contents

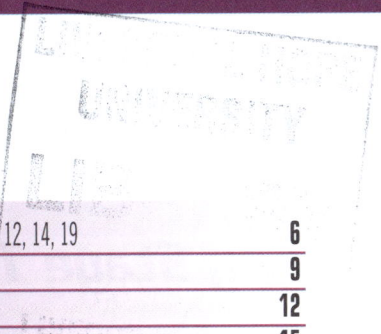

Introduction

Key Stage Two

In Key Stage Two, at your primary school, you completed a wide range of work in speaking and listening. You:

- had discussions
- worked in pairs
- made presentations to the rest of the class
- in groups or on your own

You had to think about the best way to do this, selecting and shaping what you have said.

You had to listen carefully to what was said, either in listening to other people in the class or to something on the television or radio. When asking questions, you needed to think about the best sorts of questions to ask to find out what you needed to know.

When you discussed different things in groups, listening to others was important as was putting your point across clearly, without talking over other people in the group. You all had to work together to make sure the discussion went well.

You may have taken part in drama activities, working in role to explore the feelings and ideas of other people or characters in books you were reading.

You thought about when it was necessary to speak more formally and accurately and how you needed to change the way you spoke when you did this. You might, too, have thought about how something is different when it is spoken from when it is written down.

It is quite likely that a great deal of your speaking and listening work was combined with work on reading and writing, and that it arose from other work you were doing.

Key Stage Three

At Key Stage Three, you will continue to do very similar things to those you did at Key Stage Two. You will find, though, that there will be more specific speaking and listening activities – these might not always be connected with other work you are doing. You will find, too, that you are assessed, or marked, on these activities.

At the end of each year, your work in English for the year is marked separately for reading, writing, speaking and listening. All three aspects of English are equally important. Much of your work in speaking and listening helps to improve your work in reading and writing: by discussing a subject you are going to write about, you will find you are clearer in your mind about what you want to say and are better able to organise your ideas when you come to write.

Speaking and listening, just like reading and writing, is not something you only do in English. The skills you are developing are useful in all the subjects you study. When you are listening to an account of a process in Science, it is important for you to pick out the key points; when you are discussing why something happened in Geography or History, you need to listen to what other people have to say and put your point forward effectively.

In all your work in speaking and listening, you will be thinking about how language works. You will think about the style you should use and the effect it will have on your listeners, the best choice of words and the way you shape your sentences. You will consider how to be a useful member of a group in discussion and how to make sure the discussion moves forward smoothly. You will continue to develop the skills to speak fluently and confidently and listen effectively in a wide range of situations.

Telling stories

Aims

- To structure a story that will be told to the whole class
- To discuss ways in which telling a story is different from writing a story
- To listen to and make comments on a presentation

Starter session

The following are **narrative** points from a story. You have to put them in the right order so that they can be told in the proper order.

Narrative point	Line
Ending the story	We saw something big come from...
Setting the scene	Suddenly there was a big splash...
Introducing characters	It was a dark, blustery wintry afternoon.
Building up tension	We picked up our bikes and ran
Describing the climax	My friends were messing about...
Establishing the context	So we squeezed through the park gates...

How many of you put these points in the same order? As a class, discuss whether it is possible to change the order and still produce a story that makes sense.

Introduction

Storytelling

Stories are structured, whether they are spoken aloud or read on a page. Structure helps your audience follow the narrative points in the story. An important element of a well-told story is **pace** – the speed at which you read. In a book, you can't control the speed of your reader! You can also use your voice – its tone and **volume** – to create mood.

Story consequences

Work in pairs.

1 Say a possible opening line to your partner, describing the setting. This might be, "The moon was full and cast shadows across the lawn" or "The sea was rough that day" or something similar. Your partner has to continue by giving details that introduce characters. This could be something like, "A girl stepped out of the trees" or "Three boys were sitting on the harbour wall". Continue exchanging sentences in the following sequence:

- setting the scene
- introducing characters
- establishing the context
- building up tension
- creating the climax
- ending the story

Your teacher will ask you to share your joint stories with the rest of the class who will listen carefully and jot down some notes to help you evaluate your presentation.

2 Discuss how you told your story. Ask yourself the following questions:
- Did you create an atmosphere when you described the setting and how did you do this? What words did you use to set the scene?
- Did you use Standard English or did you use slang words?
- Were you able to tell the story without hesitation or mumbling?
- How well did you pace your storytelling?

Radio drama

Divide into groups of four.
You are going to adapt a story for radio drama.
You have to make some decisions before you can begin. One of you will have to act as director.
- What will your story be about? Will it be one that you have studied in class that can be adapted for broadcast on the radio? It could be developed from the one you created in activity A or it could be a brand new one. It can be an extract from a longer story or a complete short one. But you will have to be quick!

- Are you going to tell your story through **dialogue** and speech alone or will you need a **narrator** to fill in any gaps? How much can an audience understand without being told directly?
- Will you have your characters tell the audience directly how they feel and what they are doing or will your audience get all this information from what they say to other people?
- Every person must have a role, either as character or narrator.

One of you will have to act as director and chair the meeting that makes these decisions. Remember you only have a short time so you must keep focused on these issues.

Construct the drama. It should be no longer than five minutes. Remember you will not be writing or reading from scripts so you have to jot down the key points that will guide your improvisation and keep it structured.

Perform the drama.

Evaluate the presentation: Together with the rest of the class, discuss how effective your presentation was in telling the story. Consider the following issues:

- Was the story clear and well structured?
- Were the characters effective and believable?
- If this was going to be scripted, which parts of the drama would be changed?
- Was the language used by narrator/characters appropriate for what the story is about?

Review

In this lesson you have worked informally in a pair and formally in a group to reach an agreement on making up a story and then a drama that has been presented to a wider audience. You have evaluated how effective this has been and judged the appropriateness of the language used.

Further developments ▷

Radio drama is easily available for individual and group listening both on tape and from BBC radio stations.

Storytelling tapes are also available commercially and are fun to listen to.

Book reviews

Aims

- To think about the difference between something that is spoken and something that is written down
- To think about the order in which you present your ideas, the vocabulary you choose and whether your listeners can make sense of what you say
- To play a part in discussion, deciding on key points and asking questions of members of other groups

Starter session

In groups of two or three, think about what you would want to know about a book before you decide if you want to read it. Your teacher will ask you to share these ideas with the rest of the class and will put your suggestions on the board.

Introduction

Talking about books

Despite all the other forms of entertainment available to us today, reading books is still a popular activity. Although you can read about what other people say about books, most people read those that are recommended to them by friends or people who share the same tastes.

Think of the last book you read and the reasons why you chose it. It might have been the book that your teacher asked you to read, or it might have been because you saw the film first. Alternatively, you may just have heard that it was worth reading.

The following table contains the paragraph openings from a student's book review. Match the headings to the opening line of the paragraph.

	Heading		Opening line
1	Positive point 1	A	The story basically involves...
2	Conclusion	B	Today I am going to talk about...
3	Plot summary	C	I was impressed with the way that...
4	Criticism 2	D	Overall I thought that...
5	Introduction	E	I didn't really like the...
6	Criticism 1	F	In addition I didn't...

Now think of a logical order for the pairings. Compare your ideas with those of the rest of the class. Did you all agree? Your teacher will put the correct order on the board or ask you to note it down.

To do the next part of this activity, you will need to have read a book recently!

Your teacher will ask you to choose a book you have read and take it in turns to go around the class completing each opening line in the order you have agreed on. For example, the person who starts off might say, "Today I am going to talk about 'The Amber Spyglass.'"

Next, you are going to present a **book review** to the class.

Think of a book you have recently read – this could be one you have read in class or one you have read for yourself.

You have to talk for one minute about the book. Keep to the following rules:
- Don't give away the title of the book
- Don't name any of the key characters
- Don't say what happens at the end

Present the book review to the class using only bullet points or prompt cards to remind you of your central points. The class then have to see if they can guess which book it was.

As many students as possible should present their reviews to the class.

Finally, as a class, you are going to study the difference between spoken and written language in the book reviews.

Think about the following:

- What sort of hesitation words were used, e.g. 'Um...' 'Ah...'?
- Because you were being careful not to give away too much, were you quite general? Did you use words like 'stuff', 'really good', 'all right'? Was your meaning still clear?
- Did you talk slowly or quickly? Did you start quickly and then slow down when you realised how long one minute was?
- Did you pretend to be any of the characters – using words or actions?

When you were listening to other people's book reviews, what answers did you find for the following questions:

- is there any more information you would like before you make a decision on whether to read this book?
- Are there any areas that you would like developed?
- has the reviewer justified his or her opinions concerning the book?
- what were the strengths and weaknesses of the review?

Draw up a table to analyze the different reviews. It should look something like this:

Student name	Book reviewed	Strengths	Weaknesses
David	The Amber Spyglass	Short and quick	Not enough information
Sujata	Stone Cold	Lots of detailed information	Too much hesitation in speaking

Review

You have practised summarising central points for a spoken presentation. You have also used formal language as part of a discussion.

Describing places

Aims

- To select appropriate vocabulary to create atmosphere so that listeners can conjure up a picture of what you are describing
- To listen to a talk, reflecting on what has been heard and make comments
- To identify the methods used to create an effect, in this case the words that have been chosen

Starter session

Word Tennis

In pairs, you are going to play word tennis.

Your teacher may give you a picture to look at or ask you to look out of the classroom window or around the room. One of you "serves" by giving a category to which the other responds with an appropriate description. The list on the left details the categories. The list on the right gives examples of possible responses.

Category	Possible Response
Colour:	Yellow
Lighting:	Bright
Sound:	Hums
Temperature:	Warm
Texture:	Soft
Who?	Friends
What?	Learning
Where?	Classroom

You will only have five seconds to respond to each serve or you lose the point. How long can you keep the rally going? When you have finished, discuss in pairs the "mood" the responses created.

Some of you will be asked to demonstrate your "games" to the rest of the class who will comment on the mood created by the words you have selected.

Introduction

Descriptive vocabulary

We use a lot of description when we are trying to communicate ideas to people. When we want to convey **atmosphere** and **mood**, we need to use language more imaginatively than when we are giving directions. Think about how you would tell a friend about a holiday resort you visited. What language would you use to describe the atmosphere, the mood and the general experience of being in that place?

ACTIVITY

In groups of three or four, identify an environment or a place that you are going to describe to the rest of the class. This could be somewhere that you would like to visit or have seen on television or film. You may wish to think of scenes such as a market place, a football match, a crowded shopping centre. Alternatively, you may wish to describe something less attractive.

In your groups, identify appropriate words that would describe this environment, without actually saying where it is. Using the categories from your starter session above, share them out amongst your group and expand them into sentences.

For example, student A might have the category 'colour' and might say,

"Everything seemed blue, different shades bouncing off..."

and student B, using the category 'texture' would add,

"the hard, metallic surfaces of the ship."

Student C, with the category of 'temperature' might continue,

"The biting cold of the wind produced icicles on the deck that formed into crystals under the men's feet."

You might have to practise and consider the order in which you use the categories.

Present this to the class and ask them to identify the place you are describing. Your teacher will ask the class to explain what evidence you gave them that enabled them to create the pictures they had in their heads as a result of your description.

Ask yourself whether you used the right vocabulary to create the pictures you wanted them to see.

Review

You have worked together in a group to construct a description and have focused on different types of vocabulary. You have listened to others and evaluated how well they produced pictures in your imagination.

As a class, identify which types of words were most effective in producing atmosphere, mood and feeling.

Is it better to use specific words or was it more effective when you used similes and metaphors?

Further developments ▷

Your teacher might give you some examples of description from other media:

For example, what is the difference between your verbal descriptions of a holiday destination and that of a television holiday programme or an advertisement?

Is language used differently where there are accompanying pictures?

Your teacher will ask you to look at travel brochures, travel writing and listen to radio programmes to give you examples of these differences. You might also want to look at some fiction and non-fiction texts to see how writers use language to describe environments and decide which one is more effective for you.

Describing characters

Aims

- To make your ideas clearer by talking about them
- To think about the vocabulary you choose
- To use talk as a way of exploring and expressing ideas

Starter session

Work in groups of four or five. Make lists of words that describe characters. Your teacher will give you one of the following categories:

Descriptive words	examples
Adjectives that describe personal characteristics	happy, sad, intelligent, kind
Nouns that describe occupations	doctor, builder, architect, cowboy
Adjectives that describe physical characteristics	large, thin, spindly
Adjectives that define gender/race/age	man, woman, Asian, Caucasian, young, old
Adjectives that define ability and health	athletic, differently abled

While you are collecting these words, think about what attitudes are suggested by them if you use them to describe a person.

You will either write these on large sheets of paper that your teacher will pin up on the wall or you will share them with the class for the teacher to write on the board.

Now, divide into pairs or groups of three. Your teacher will allocate you a word from each group. You only have five minutes. Can you produce a description of that character from the words that you have been given?

Share your descriptions with the rest of the class. As a class, discuss what kind of characters you have created from those words. Have you produced **stereotypes**? Have you thought about people you might know? Listen to the presentations of the rest of the class. Have your students produced original characters? Are these characters recognisable, humorous, believable?

Introduction

Describing characters

Comedians often create characters as part of their set routine. Your teacher may be able to show you some extracts from comics such as Les Dawson who is famous for his portrayal of older Northern women, or an extract from Harry Enfield and Cathy Burke's Kevin and Perry. Situation comedy relies upon constructing stereotypes of characters that are immediately recognisable. You may be able to recall some of them or even look at some extracts from programmes. As a class, you will discuss how the actors use language, gestures and silence to suggest characteristics that are familiar to their audiences and create humour.

ACTIVITY

On a piece of paper, each of you will write a brief description of a character that might be used in a situation comedy. For example you might describe the difficult adolescent, such as Kevin or you might consider the grumpy old man, such as Victor Meldrew. Give your piece of paper to your teacher who will shuffle them and hand one to each of you randomly.

Work in groups of four or five. Look at the description you have been given and consider how that character might use language. For example, characters who are trying to "keep up appearances" frequently attempt to use quite formal language, but don't use it correctly. You may remember Del Boy from 'Only Fools and Horses', who does this.

In your groups can you hold a conversation in your roles as these characters?

You will be given the opportunity to try this out and your teacher will ask you to demonstrate your work to the rest of the class.

After each performance, the class should consider the kind of language each character has used and what this shows us about the character. You will need to think:

- Are there particular phrases that the character has used?
- What kind of **register** has each character used and is it appropriate for that character?
- Is there specific **vocabulary** that is associated with this character?
- Does the language show the point of view of the character?
- Have you produced a stereotypical character?

Review

What have you learned through this activity?

As a class, evaluate how you have constructed characters through their use of language.

You might want to consider how we use stereotypes and **caricatures** for comedy.

Consider how we form opinions of people through their use of language.

Evaluate how your own use of language creates an impression on people who do not know you very well.

Further developments ▷

Keep a list of comedy stereotypes, and update it when you see new programmes. For example, make a note of the characteristics of family members in situation comedies and compare and contrast between different programmes. How often do the same characteristics in characters appear in different programmes?

Role playing

Aims

- To take on a role to explore different situations
- To broaden the way you speak by taking on different roles in a variety of contexts
- To consider carefully how successful your own and other students' presentations are

Starter session

In groups of four, greet each other using as many different types of tone, register, vocabulary and **structure** as possible. This could range from "Good morning" to "Hi! How you doing?" How many greetings can your group produce? When you have finished, as a group, complete a table like this:

Speaker	Spoken to	Context	Greeting	Type
Jo	Terri	Met on the bus	"Watcha!"	Informal, familiar
Jo	Mr Jones	Registration	"Morning sir."	Formal, respectful

How many versions did you manage in the time limit?

Have you noticed how you even change the way you use language with the same person, depending on where you are when you speak to them? For example, if you are discussing something in a lesson with a fellow student, do you use the same language as when you are at lunch together?

Introduction

Speaking and listening context

The same person uses different types of language, depending on the **roles** that they take.

For example, as your parents' child, do you use language differently when speaking to them than you do when you are speaking to another adult in your family?

When you speak to your teacher, do you use language differently from when you are having a conversation with a visitor to your school?

ACTIVITY

In groups of four, draw up a list of the many different roles you take in the course of a week. You might want to use the following headings:

- family roles
- friendship roles
- work roles as a student or pupil to the teacher

Each group will give this list to the teacher who will share them with the rest of the class.

You will then be asked to identify a **speaking and listening context**. This refers to the roles taken on by people who are talking to each other, the reason why they are talking or listening and the way they use language. As a class, group the roles into speaking and listening contexts. Think about how the roles might make a difference to the kind of language that is used.

Friend and friend:

making an apology

trying to arrange an evening out

telling friend some gossip

complaining about a teacher/parent

pointing out a mistake

asking for some information

Think about whether you talk to friends differently and why. How does your language change from one friend to another and in different situations?

In pairs, take a role each and use language to achieve the purpose you have been given. For example, one of you might be a friend making an apology to another friend for something. When you have finished, comment on the other person's use of language and how successful they were in achieving what they set out to do. What was the difference between the use of language in the formal and informal context? You might want to think about:

tone of voice   clarity of expression   the attitude shown

kinds of sentences used: long, short, simple, complicated

the kind of vocabulary used   gesture and body language

Look at the following roles and situations – they might be familar:

Pupil and teacher:

pupil asking teacher for help   pupil asking teacher for extra time

pupil making an excuse   pupil pointing out teacher mistake

pupil explaining situation   pupil informing teacher about incident

Think about whether you use language differently depending upon who the teacher is. Would you talk to your form teacher the way you would speak to the head teacher?

Child and parent:

child asking parent for money   child making an excuse

child telling parent about school   child explaining situation

child pointing out parental mistake   child trying to persuade parent

These sorts of situations are probably very familiar and you might want to talk about how you would handle them. Have you thought about how the way you use language determines whether or not you get your own way?

You and a familiar adult	You and an unfamiliar adult
asking to get a ball out of their garden	telling them about your school
asking for help	describing an art/DT/drama project

Think about which adults, other than teachers and family, you speak with. Make a list of them and discuss how you use language with them.

Your teacher will give you two speaking and listening contexts from this list or from the lists you shared with the class. One will be formal and the other more informal.

Get into groups of four and take on roles in different contexts. This time, one pair listens to the other pair and feeds back how successful they think they were in achieving their aims. They should comment on the use of language and how that affected the result of the conversation. Take it in turns, making sure each pair has at least one turn at a conversation and evaluation

You will feed back to the rest of the class and should prepare the following:

- A short evaluation of how successful the conversation was in achieving what it set out to do
- How the conversation could have been more successful and how one or other of the people involved could have overcome problems by using language in a particular way

Review

At the end of the activity, all the class should have had a turn at exploring paired conversations in different roles and contexts and evaluated your own and each others' performances.

As a whole class, decide which of the conversations were the most successful and try to identify what features of language made them work well.

Moral dilemmas

Aims

- To listen carefully and think about the main points you have heard
- To say whether you are for or against a point of view, giving relevant reasons why
- To listen carefully to other people's views, sometimes making changes to your ideas as a result
- To take on a role in order to explore a situation
- To use drama methods to work out what to do in a situation

Starter session

Spend five minutes thinking about situations that arise where people of your age have to choose between right and wrong. The situations can be real or imaginary. Here are some ideas to get you started:

I saw a girl from year 9 write graffiti in the toilets. It was about a teacher.

"I broke my mum's antique clock by accident. I have a younger sister who is just beginning to walk and mum won't be as angry if I say it was her. Shall I lie? Should I say something?

(At the end of this section, there are some more 'dilemmas' and sources of advice, in case you are stuck for ideas.)

Write your ideas down and hand them to your teacher.

Next, write down a list of people or organisations you might approach for advice and hand that to your teacher.

Situation	Source of advice

Your teacher will now share your ideas with the whole class and write a list on the board. Your teacher will then summarise some of these situations and either jot them down on the board or ask you to make a note of them.

Work in groups of four or five and consider the lists.

Are there some situations that need specific advice? Match the list of advisors to the list of problems and discuss why you have chosen specific advisors to help with certain problems or **dilemmas**. This list might look like this:

Situation	Source of advice
1. Saw a girl write graffiti in the toilets. Do I tell?	My best friend/friend of that girl
2. Broke something, own up/ blame someone else?	Member of the family/friend

Discuss the situations and make a decision about whose advice you would ask for each of them.

Share your decisions with the rest of the class. Do you all agree? Why are there differences?

In case you cannot think of anything, here are some dilemmas with which you might be familiar:

1 I know that my friend has had an occasional cigarette. His mother is very anti-smoking because a close family member died of lung cancer. Should I interfere?

2 A boy in year 11 is taking money from two year 8 boys. I saw them at break. Should I mention it to someone?

3 I didn't do my homework on Wednesday and I knew the teacher would be angry. My brother did it for me and I got commended for it. I know that some people in the class worked really hard on the project. Should I own up?

4 Some year 10 pupils are bullying my friend. They give out bad looks and say things; sometimes they sound as if they're threatening but it's difficult to say what they're doing. My friend says it doesn't matter. Should I see someone about it?

5 I borrowed my brother's new bike and scratched it quite badly. Should I own up and tell him or pretend that I know nothing about it?

6 All my friends are going to a youth club disco but my parents think I'm too young to stay out late. One of my friends has offered to let me stay over after the disco and my parents need not know how late it finished. What should I do?

7 All my friends have the latest trainers, but my family can't afford to pay for such things. I don't want to be the only one without them. My friend says that s/he knows how to get them really cheap. Should I ask my parents again?

8 My best friend from primary school and I ended up in the same class. S/he doesn't get on with some of the new friends that I have made and she said that she feels left out when I spend time with them. But I don't want to lose these new friends. What do I do?

9 I don't like going to my new friend's house because her/his mum often shouts a lot and it makes me feel embarrassed. My mum likes me to go round because she doesn't get back from work until late and it helps her out. I don't want to make things difficult. What can I do?

Sources of advice:

Friends   Teacher   Parents

Brother/sister   Priest or church   Magazine

Prefect   Other family   Specialist agency

Police   Youth worker   Social worker

Neighbour

ACTIVITY

Work in groups of six. Your teacher will give you a problem. Organise yourselves into pairs. One of you takes the part of the person with the problem and the other becomes the person suggesting what should be done, or 'advisor'. You should end up with THREE different sources of advice. For example, for problem 4, you might seek the advice of a parent, another friend and a teacher. How would the advice differ? Why would you not ask your parents' advice for dilemma 9?

Spend ten minutes maximum on the role-play with one of you playing the advisor selected, using the sort of language you think that person would use.

Go back into your group of six. The three who have sought the advice should summarise and explain the advice each was given to the whole group. The "advisors" should listen carefully and check whether their advice has been summarised accurately and whether good listening has occurred. How good was the advice given? Would the person with the dilemma have taken this advice?

The whole group then discusses why the advice might differ between the advisors and discuss the different viewpoints people in these roles might have.

As a group of six, come up with a decision as to how to resolve the dilemma.

Review

Choose three people from the group to tell the rest of the class what happened. One person explains and develops the problem and another summarises the advice given. The last person explains what action occurred as a result.

If there is time, it would be interesting to have a whole-class discussion on any one of these problems and the solutions offered.

Further developments ▷

Literature is often about problems, either personal or professional. Think about a book or play you have studied recently. Are there similar problems that have arisen in them? It is likely that some of the literature you are studying contains these dilemmas and this would be a good way of discussing them.

Giving and receiving instructions

Aims

- To give clear instructions that are helpfully ordered and connected

Starter session

Look at these instructions showing you how to make a cup of tea: they are obviously in the wrong order.

- Put teabags in the teapot
- Switch it off when it boils
- After a few minutes pour the tea into a cup or mug
- Fill the kettle with water
- Put milk in a cup or mug

Put these in the right order.

Discuss how difficult or easy this was.

Work in pairs. Sit back to back. One of you will have a pen and a blank piece of paper. One will give instructions to the other about how to draw a shape or write a word without mentioning the name of the shape or the letters and word. You will need to be very clear and explicit and get the sequence right. Share your results with the class.

Work out how successful the instructions were and explore why some worked and some did not.

Introduction

Clear instructions

Giving clear instructions is an important skill. You are going to work together to develop this skill.

Work in pairs. Take it in turns. One of you will give instructions to the other who will follow them exactly to undertake one of the following activities:

- putting on and tying a tie
- putting on a shoe and doing up the laces
- changing a cartridge in a fountain pen

In your pairs discuss how effective the instructions were. How difficult is it to explain something like this to someone, when you are used to doing it automatically?

On a piece of paper write down a simple task that can be undertaken in the classroom. This could be something like getting up and switching on the light or putting a piece of paper in the rubbish bin. Hand it to your teacher.

You will work in different pairs for this activity.

Your teacher will shuffle the bits of paper and allocate a task to one person in the pair. That student will give instructions to the other without telling them what it is that they will be doing. Exchange your paper instructions with another pair and change places so that both of you give and follow instructions. Were better instructions given this time? Was it more difficult following the instructions when you did not know what it was that you were doing?

Review

Your teacher will ask some of you to demonstrate your instructions to the rest of the class. Your teacher will choose some of you to demonstrate this activity with a new task from the suggestions you have come up with.

As a class, evaluate whether these instructions were successful and why.

Further developments ▷

Many programmes on television give instructions. These include gardening, cookery, home improvements, hair and make-up programmes. Watch one of these and discuss what sort of language is used and how dependent the instructions are on visual information and demonstration.

Giving and receiving directions

Aims

- To think about the order of what you are going to say and the vocabulary you choose so that your listeners can make sense of what you say
- To look at how a familiar way of speaking is organised and at what the particular features are of this

Starter session

Working in pairs, write on a piece of paper all the words that you would use for giving directions. You can include the words next to the exercise. Share your work with the rest of the class and the teacher will write them on the board.

Either in pairs or as a whole class **brainstorm** other words that are needed for directions. These are more likely to be 'movement' words, verbs that instruct, such as *turn, move, go*. These are called **imperatives**.

In pairs, match them up. Do some words go better with certain imperatives? You should share these with the whole class. For example, how many of you paired *turn* with *right*, rather than *move left*, or *turn forward*. As a class, discuss why we pair these words as we do.

Over there.

Introduction

Giving directions

Giving directions is an important part of speaking and listening. The speaker has to be very precise and clear if the directions are to make sense and the listener has to concentrate and visualise the movement. You will use a different sort of language when you do this from that you used when you described characters and places.

ACTIVITY **A**

Understanding directions

Your teacher will choose two of you in turn and tell one of you secretly where s/he wants you to direct the other pupil. Your job is to give the other pupil a series of directions to get him or her to the place your teacher has thought of. Don't take short cuts and say, "To the front of the room", but direct them around the obstacles. After you've given the directions, the other pupil has to remember your words and find out where they should be.

As a whole class discuss and evaluate the success of the directions:

Were the directions clear and precise?

Did the listener follow the directions or was there a loss of concentration.

Was there difficulty in remembering the directions?

Think about how the structure of the directions can help the listener understand what is being said.

Right.

In front.

Write a **location** on a piece of paper and give it to your teacher. This could be somewhere in the school or somewhere more imaginative, such as Mars. Your teacher will hand out the locations to the class.

Work in pairs. Don't tell your partner where they are going and give directions to get to the stated location. You will have to start with "Get up and …". Your partner has to listen very carefully and visualise where they are going. If they are uncertain, they may ask questions which you answer, but you must not state the destination. When you have finished, if they guess correctly where they are, you have both been successful in giving and receiving directions!

Your teacher may ask you to direct the whole class to a fantastical location and award points for the first person to realise where they are going!

Review

You have worked in pairs and as a whole class in giving directions. You have used specific language to do this effectively. Discuss as a class the type of language you have used. Your teacher may jot down points on the board to help you focus on the different vocabulary and structures that you used when speaking. What type of language helped the listener follow the directions best?

Further developments ▷

There are a number of areas that could be explored through this activity. For example, pupils might like to look at types of words that are used in giving directions and **develop their vocabulary**, particularly with **prepositions**.

As a **research activity**, pupils could be asked to look at how directions are used in different genres. For example when are directions used in travel writing? Are there any instances in fiction where giving directions has been used to create humour?

Giving and receiving directions *[extension material]*

Aims

- To look at how directions are organised and what the typical features are
- To think about the difference between spoken and written language

Starter session

Simon Says

Your teacher will perform as Simon and will instruct you to perform simple movements. You will have to listen carefully because the last person to perform the movement is out of the game. If you have time, the last person in the game could be Simon and lead the class again.

Introduction

Clear directions

You have given and received directions to perform certain tasks. How different is this from giving and receiving instructions? The language that you use is similar as you will need to use prepositions [placing words] and imperatives [verbal commands]. We often use directions for purposes other than helping someone physically get to a specific place and use different types of language.

Get into pairs. One of you read these directions to the other:

> If you go straight down this rather bumpy hill that's going up. Just behind there's a sweet shop where my aunt used to get her papers in the morning. She was nice my aunt, she used to wear strange clothes and stuff though. There's a garage on the corner, it might be a car show room though and it's all lit up at night. My neighbour's always complaining about it because she says the light shines in her bedroom window.

Discuss whether these directions help someone reach their destination. Pick out all the information that is unclear and not necessary. Is anything in this list helpful? Would there be any occasion for which this language is appropriate?

Swap places and read these directions to the other:

> I was born in Chobham. Somebody had to be. To reach this sleepy hollow set somewhere between the 1950s and the 21st century, you have to journey back through mock cottage dwellings posing as the bolt holes of stressed executives and their wives who people-carrier their offspring to school. Ever circulating, you need to weave your way onto the latest development in circular car parks, through routes of urban boxes, sheltering behind tall elms that reach up, almost desperately in their worship of the distant sky. The years clock back like a demented time-machine whirring through memories of early adulthood, adolescence and childhood; events, characters, sounds and sensations fill the space left between then and now until the sign appears, miles out of the village; as if the community itself were reaching out, poaching space that really is not theirs.

Would these directions get you to the village? Do you think this language is intended to *physically* direct you to the village? In your pairs, look to see if you can find any differences between this extract and the one above. Consider the **purpose** of both of them and why the listener might be interested. Is it possible that one would be spoken and one would be written?

Share your ideas with the class.

The language used tells the listener your purpose. If you were actually giving directions, the extracts above would be totally unsuitable.

If you are giving directions to a location, the listener has to imagine the route and this requires concentration. If the directions contain a lot of information that is not necessary, or is unclear, it will not be easy for the listener to imagine the route.

A map works as a visual direction but not everyone is good at reading one! In this activity, you will be using maps to give directions.

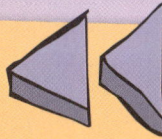

Spend five minutes making a map from the list of suggestions below. Alternatively, your teacher may give you one.

Suggestions:

- a map of the school
- a map of the local area
- a road map of any area.
- a fictional map such as that printed in the beginning of *The Hobbit*, or *Lord of the Rings*
- a map you construct yourself to suit the location of any literature you might be studying
- an atlas [if you want to be really adventurous!]

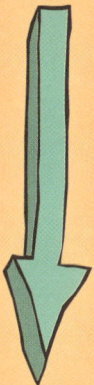

In pairs, identify where you are located on the map at the beginning of the journey and your destination. Take it in turns to give directions to the other.

After each set of directions, decide whether there was an easier route.

Was sufficient description given?

Was it easy to follow?

To make it more difficult, listen to the directions without knowing the identity of the destination and see whether you end up in the right place!

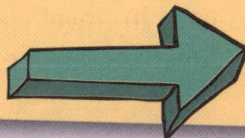

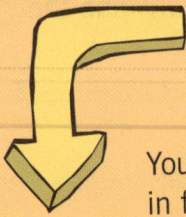

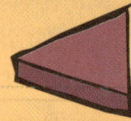

Your teacher will ask some of you to give directions in front of the class. Discuss what kind of language you used:

As well as using specific words, did you change the way you spoke?

Did you use particular sentence structures?

Did you listen to your partner to see if they understood you?

How did your partner show you that they did or did not understand?

Did they use gestures, facial expressions or give verbal clues?

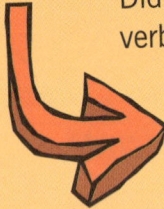

Review

As a class, discuss what you achieved and evaluate how well you spoke and listened. Consider how language is structured differently depending upon the purpose of the speaker and listener. Discuss the differences between spoken and written language. Your teacher may construct a **spidergram** on the board to help you take notes on this.

Further developments ▷

As a research activity, look at how directions are used in different genres. For example when are directions used in travel writing? Are there any instances in fiction where giving directions has been used to create humour?

Arguing your case

Aims

- To make your ideas clearer by talking about them
- To play a particular part in a discussion, saying why you are for or against a point of view or idea and giving reasons for this
- To work together in a group to test out and weigh up ideas

Starter session

It makes me mad!

On a piece of paper, describe something that you dislike. This can be an issue, an object or a famous person. It cannot be someone known by only a few or someone in the school.

Hand the pieces of paper to your teacher. As a class, organise the dislikes into categories. For example, you may find it useful to divide them into people and things or school issues such as uniform and toilets and wider issues such as experiments on animals and vandalism. Your teacher will jot these down on the board.

Subject	Category	
	Person / thing	issue

Divide into groups of four: each of you has 100 points. Go through the list and decide which four dislikes are the most important. You can allocate some of your points to each of them. As you allocate, explain your preferences to the rest of the group.

Nominate a spokesperson to feed your conclusions back to the rest of the class.

Introduction

Argument has a definite purpose: it suggests that reasons are put forward to support or oppose a **proposition**. It is different from **persuasion** which has a definite purpose of changing someone's mind or making someone do something. A good argument, of course, can often be persuasive. Although the word also describes a disagreement or a quarrel, in the following activity, you are going to construct an argument.

ACTIVITY

Points of view

You will work in a group of four. Identify a topic that interests you. This may be one of the dislikes that you discussed in the starter activity, or it could be a new topic. Divide your group into two pairs; each pair will take a **point of view** that opposes the other.

In pairs discuss how you will construct your argument. Brainstorm key points and jot them down. For example if your topic is school uniform and you are arguing in favour of keeping it, you might jot down these points:

- Don't have to worry about what to wear
- Keeps everyone the same
- Identifies which school you attend
- Not affected by fashion

Discuss the order in which your argument would use these points.

A good argument normally predicts what the opposition might suggest and is ready for it. Guess what the opposing view might include as points and construct a table. It might look something like this:

Topic: School uniform

For	Against
Keeps everyone the same	Allows self-expression and freedom
Identifies which school you attend	We are individuals and should dress so

As you discuss how you are going to construct your argument, remember you can use elements of humour that can be persuasive. For example for the point regarding fashion, you might want to tell your audience that the benefit of school uniform is that it stays <u>out</u> of fashion. You will need to make a note of where you want to make a particular statement.

When you have finished, go back into your group of four. Compare your grids. Did you successfully predict the points your "opposition" made? Go back into your pairs and allocate points for each other to use as part of your "joint" argument. Return to your group of four and present your joint arguments to each other. You should use your table as a **prompt** rather than writing down everything you are going to say.

Review

You have presented reasons for liking and disliking something and learned how to construct a point of view.

Your teacher will ask some of you to present your joint arguments to the rest of the class who will decide who they think is the most convincing.

Arguing your case
[extension material]

Aims

- To think about the way you present your ideas so that your listeners can make sense of what you say
- To say why you are for or against a point of view, giving your reasons
- To listen carefully to what you have heard so you can ask clear and relevant questions

Starter session

Argument bingo

You will use the tables that you constructed in the last unit. Swap them around so that you all have different tables. Your teacher will ask a member of the class to talk through a point on his or her table. It must not be read out; the point should be used to help talk. The rest of the class will listen carefully while looking at their tables. The person who has a table on the same subject has to respond with the opposing point being made. The points should not be read out but put into different words. The points should be ticked off as they are mentioned. This should be continued until all the points are used. The teacher will then select another subject until you have all had a chance.

Introduction

Creating a debate

Arguments can be presented in opposition to each other. This produces an either/or situation where a listener is presented with two views. This happens at the beginning of a debate, or in a legal case when a lawyer presents a point of view. To help the listeners identify the argument with which they agree, the speakers presenting the point of view have to **debate** or *discuss*. You have already undertaken a number of activities in which you used discussion but it was likely to be informal and not very organised. Formal discussions and debates have structures.

Mini debates

You can use the tables you made in the last unit or think of a different subject. In a group of four, take opposing views on a subject you all want to discuss. In pairs, discuss what points you will make that will support your view and share them between you. Write each point briefly on a small piece of paper or a card. These will be called "prompt cards" and may look like this:

> Pro-uniform
> Makes everyone equal

You may wish to number these cards in the order in which you would present them.

In your pair, one of you will use the prompt cards to make your presentation as an opening to the debate. You need to time yourself; your speech should be no longer than three minutes. A member of the other pair will respond by offering their speech. It is usual for the person in favour of an idea or a motion to go first so that the person against can respond. This happens in a legal case when the prosecution go first, presenting their argument, followed by the presentation by the defence.

When the cases have been presented, the second person in the pair will respond to the opposing presentation.

Review

Your teacher will ask some of you to present your 'debates' to the rest of the class who will respond as an audience.

The main speaker for the motion will give their presentation to the class using only their cards as prompts. The main speaker opposing will then give theirs. The second speaker for the motion will address the issues of the first speaker of the opposition and will be followed by the second speaker opposing the motion.

The class should listen carefully to the arguments offered and must be ready to ask questions.

When all the questions have been asked, the teacher will ask the class to vote on whose argument has convinced them.

Asking questions

Aims

- To ask clear and relevant questions
- To give clear and careful answers
- To listen carefully and think about the main points of what you have heard
- To work together in a group to solve problems, testing out and weighing up ideas
- To consider how successful you and other students are in your presentations

Starter session A

What's my job?

Write down the name of a job or profession on a piece of paper and hand it to your teacher. You might include jobs such as builder, baker, teacher, doctor, salesperson etc.

Your teacher will shuffle them and hand one back to each member of the class.

Get into groups of four. You have ten minutes to complete the task.

Three members of the group will ask the fourth questions to find out what their job or profession is. You must not state what it is but give as much information as possible in response to their questions to help them guess. You cannot offer information that is not asked for by their questions.

Did you manage to get all four jobs in the ten minutes? What questions helped you best in getting the information you needed to help you guess.

Is it possible to sort out these questions into different types?
Your teacher will ask a member of the group to feed back to the whole class your evaluation of what was successful and what was not.

Starter session B

Swap all the "jobs" around and work in pairs. You have five minutes for this activity. Each of you will ask the other a question in turn. The response can only be 'Yes' or 'No' or 'Maybe'. How quickly can you identify the job? Who got the correct answer first and what questions did you ask that helped?

As a class discuss what are useful questions when trying to gain information?

Introduction

Verbal charades

In order to get the information you want, you often have to ask the right questions.

"Twenty Questions" was a famous radio show where guests had to guess the identity of an object. They started by defining whether it was animal, vegetable or mineral and then broke questions down into categories such as "Does it help humanity?" "Is it a service?" "Is it a building?" You have to listen carefully to the answers as they will help you decide the next useful question.

ACTIVITY

On a piece of paper, write down the name of an object of a person under the following categories

- Famous people
- Famous buildings
- Famous books and films
- Well known television programmes
- Countries
- Sportspeople

Hand them to your teacher who will shuffle them and redistribute them amongst you.

Divide into groups of four.

Your teacher will tell you which category you will start off with. Three members of the group will ask questions of the fourth to identify the name of the person, object, country etc under the category. They will take it in turns to ask their questions, listening carefully to the responses so that they do not waste time. Although the fourth person cannot give information that is not asked for, they must tell the truth and be as clear and specific as possible.

After five minutes, the teacher will tell you to stop.

As a class find out which groups managed to get their answers in the time. Discuss how they did it and what kind of questions helped to get the right answer. If you were not successful, did you waste time asking unhelpful or unfocused questions?

Your teacher will then ask you to repeat the exercise using someone else to answer the questions, until each of you has had the opportunity to respond to questions.

If you have time, brainstorm which techniques worked best and see whether you can draw up a set of categories in which the questions could be grouped.

Nominate a spokesperson to feed back your conclusions to the rest of the class.

Review

You have had the opportunity to ask different types of questions for different purposes. You have also evaluated the success of your questioning and identified a pattern or categories of questions. Feedback your conclusions to the rest of the class.

Telling stories for different audiences

Aims

- To talk individually within a given context, trying out different moods, tones and paces of delivery in order to achieve a particular effect.
- To think about the different ways in which information can be put across, according to who is speaking, who they are talking to and what they are talking about
- To listen to and assess the use of these verbal effects in others

Starter session A

Using the phrase, "on the way to school", each student will quickly finish the sentence as an opening to a story. For example, student A may say, "On the way to school, I met an alien". The next student may suggest, "On the way to school, I noticed that it had begun to rain." Each member of the class should be able to give a different ending to the sentence. Discuss, as a whole class, whether it is possible to group your responses into categories. For example, would you group "I met an alien" with this response, "…I had a sudden idea", or with "…a space ship landed on the bus stop"? Discuss what the responses share in common.

Starter session B

Go round the class finishing this sentence: "Sorry, I haven't got my homework because…." You can use any excuse you like. These could be serious, such as "I brought the wrong bag to school", or fantastical, such as "A gorilla jumped down from a tree and ate it".

As a class, discuss the kind of stories you told. With your teacher's help, group them into categories. Your categories could be genre-based (for example, fantasy, comedy) or based more on tone (sarcasm, humour, politeness).

Introduction

Addressing your audience

Stories are told differently depending upon whom they are for and what you hope to achieve. What story would you use to convince your teacher not to give you a detention? Consider whether you would need to tell it in a certain way to create an effect on your teacher (your **audience**), such as making them laugh or trying to make them feel sorry for you?

ACTIVITY

1 As a class, list the types of audience that you might want to address on a typical school day. This could include the following although you could probably think of a lot more:

- Parents
- Brothers/sisters
- Friends
- Teachers
- Bus drivers

Then make a list of the kinds of **purposes** you might want to achieve. This might include the following:

- Making an excuse
- Creating humour
- Persuading someone to do something for you
- Creating sympathy

Finally make a list of **tones** that you might use for these purposes. Include thoughts about pace and delivery. Your list might include:

- Sad, mournful or pathetic= quiet, slow
- Confident= rapid, louder, lots of eye contact
- Uncertain and tentative= quiet, repetitive
- Sarcastic= hurried, under breath, less formal

Your teacher will help you with this.

2 You will have ten minutes to do this activity. In groups of four, make a table that links audience, purpose and tone similar to this one:

Audience	Purpose	Tone and pace
Teacher	excuse for not handing in homework	• respectful, serious, sad • slow, controlled

Share your ideas with the rest of the class and discuss why certain tones are more suitable to achieve your purpose with certain audiences. What did you discover?

3 Your teacher will now give each group a purpose to achieve, together with four different audiences taken from your original list. In your groups of four, take it in turns to tell your story to the others, each of you targeting a different audience. The listeners have to adopt the role of the target audience and decide whether the story, pace and tone were appropriate for that audience. You could jot down notes in an assessment sheet, something like this:

	Successful points	Things to improve
Story	good, believable excuses	
Tone	appropriately formal	
Pace		slow down! you don't sound like you mean it

Finally, decide whether the speaker has been successful in achieving their purpose.

Review

Each group should share their findings with the rest of the class. Discuss whether time and place might make a difference to the tone you would use when talking to the same audience. Your teacher will help you draw some general conclusions.

Role playing a traffic accident

Aims

- To give an explanation of an event, linking words with images
- To use role-play to examine different perspectives

Starter session

As a class, think about situations where people might have seen the same incident in different ways, where there could have been several different versions given of the same event.

Introduction

Different perspectives

There are often different stories or versions of events. These can vary according to **perspective** (where the person is or what they believe) and purpose (what the person wants to achieve). In Activity A, you will be using group discussion to construct an account of a realistic road traffic accident. You will have to work together to reach a conclusion within a time limit. In Activity B, you will take on various roles, using appropriate language to achieve your purposes.

Divide into groups of four. Your aim is to design and construct a road traffic accident. For this you will need to devise a simple road map showing the road, any notable landmarks that will help identify the location and any intersections or obstacles. Once you have done this, discuss how a real accident could happen. Could there be more than one version of what happened? For example, did the cyclist wobble into the car or did the car slide into the cyclist? Decide how many witnesses there might be and where they might be located on the map.

On a sheet of paper, write down the basic facts that are indisputable. For example:

● The road was wet
● The cyclist was knocked off the bicycle
● A car was involved
● Two witnesses saw the accident. They were standing at different locations.

Decide amongst you who, if anyone, was to blame and do not tell anyone else.

When you have finished, hand in the map and the list of basic facts to your teacher.

Your teacher will redistribute the maps and facts so that groups are given accidents designed by others.

Allocate the following roles to members of the group:

● People involved in the accident
● Witnesses
● Police

Look at the map and the facts as a group and make sure that you all understand what happened in the accident. Discuss why people might have had different ideas about what happened. Consider how each person might interpret the facts. Assume that the purpose of those involved in the accident is to avoid being blamed. Assume that the witnesses' purpose is to give as honest account as possible.

Role-play what happened after the accident. It should be 'directed' by the police taking **verbal** statements from each of the participants and from the witness or witnesses. Each character needs to *explain* their version of the events:

- give a chronological account
- give reasons for their actions

As a group, discuss how the police asked questions. Were they good enough to get more facts? Were the answers clear and precise?

Think up and write down alternative versions of the questions, which you think would have achieved clearer answers. How did the participants manage to shift any blame away from themselves? How effective were the witnesses?

The student playing the police officer should decide whether to prosecute someone for what happened based on the evidence s/he gained from their questioning.

Review

The student playing the police officer will give a brief account of the accident to the rest of the class together with their findings. The group who designed the accident will announce whether the officer has made the right decision. Discuss as a class why similar or different decisions were made.

Desert Island Game

Aims

- To talk in Standard English, thinking of ways of persuading the people you are speaking to
- To play different parts in discussion, such as helping the group to reach an agreement and building on other people's contributions
- To think about how you could have improved your performance in taking part in a discussion

Starter session

As a class, brainstorm some circumstances that would leave you stranded… This could be a shipwreck or a plane crash. Decide on one.

Each member of the class now names an object that they have saved. You can only name one and it should be different for each student. It must be an item you would have with you in your chosen senario. Your teacher will write the name of the object on the board. From the list, each student should choose five items that they think might be useful on the island.

Introduction

Making difficult choices

We often have to work out solutions with other people. Speaking and listening is an important skill in achieving a successful outcome. You need to think about the other person's point of view, imagine how they feel and what they might want to achieve. When you **negotiate**, try to get as close to the other person's viewpoint as possible while keeping what is important from your own. In this activity, you will all have a different point of view and will try to reach a **compromise**.

Get into groups of five. Think about how you might have been stranded on the island. Decide which reason you like best, and use it as the basis for this activity.

1 The group will have 25 objects that have survived with you. Imagine that there is a storm and 10 objects are washed away. Decide between you which of the objects you would most want to have been saved and the reasons for keeping these. You may have to give up some of the objects you chose, if you feel other people's objects would be of more use.

2 There is now a hurricane and you have had to struggle to save your possessions. You only manage to save 5. Which ones would you most want to keep? Argue your case for keeping what is most valuable to you and most useful to the whole group.

3 Tell the rest of the class what happened and how you were stranded on the island. Describe the objects you decided to keep and the reasons for this. You need to put your ideas across clearly in order to convince the class that you made the right choices. Make sure you are grammatically correct in what you say and use a formal style.

4 Get back into your groups. Think about a problem which could arise which would cause conflict in the group. One of the group might be thought to be taking more of their share of the food; some of you might think not everyone is 'pulling their weight' or there might be a clash of personalities.

5 Role-play the situation where you discuss what is happening. Make sure each member of the group has a chance to put forward his or her viewpoint and try to reach an agreement about what should be done to solve the problem.

Alternative activity for a longer session

In this activity, you will be asked to construct an **oral** diary in your groups. Your teacher will ask you to construct a "story", as you did in Unit 1, for each day that you are stranded on the island. You may be given obstacles or issues to deal with by other students or by your teacher, that your group has to use in their story. Because there are different viewpoints, you might be asked individually to tell your stories to show those different perspectives.

Review

You have spent some time in groups, negotiating possible conflicting viewpoints and reaching compromises that are best for the good of the group. You have concluded by acting out a conflict scenario in which one of you has to act as someone who helps you all to agree. Your teacher might ask some of you to act out this activity in front of the class.

As a class, evaluate the success of the process by which you came to an agreement. Consider how language was used to help each member of the group understand the viewpoints of others and reach a compromise. Evaluate your own performance. Were you prepared to listen to others' ideas and feelings? Did you put across your own feelings and thoughts successfully? Were you able to be assertive and confident without being bullying or unwilling to listen to others?

On the board, brainstorm areas for improvement. Make a note of the top two points which apply most directly to your own performance.

The Travel Game

Aims

- To pay careful attention to what you are listening to in order to identify key information and think about how good you are at doing this
- To play different parts in discussion, such as helping the group to agree and reporting back the main points that come up

Starter session

In silence, for one minute, think of where you would like to go on holiday. You have enough money and time to go wherever you want. Note your dream destinations on the board.

Introduction

It is easier to remember what some people say than it is for others. Good speakers tend to talk in a way that is clear, relevant and linked to the subject being discussed.

ACTIVITY **A**

Now work in pairs. Student A explains his/her preferences to Student B who listens and does not interrupt or offer any comments. Student A should refer to the following questions:

- Where is the holiday? Why do you wish to go?
- What do you hope to gain from the holiday?
- What do you hope to do and why?
- What does this choice says about you as a person?

Student B has to listen very carefully and not take notes but sum up the main points and report them back to Student A. Change places. Student B should now talk without interruption to Student A who should listen carefully.

Swap partners with another pair. Sum up for your new partner what your old partner told you about their preferred holiday.

Your teacher will ask some of you to report back to the class what one of your partners told you about their preferred holiday. That partner will evaluate the accuracy of what you have said. You should think about <u>why</u> differences occurred.

Listening to different points of view

Work in groups of four. Three of you will take the role of a specific character that will be given to you by your teacher. The fourth member of the group will act as a travel agent whose purpose is to sell a suitable holiday that all three characters can agree on.

These characters will not be known to the travel agent and may be very different. For example the groups of three might consist of the following combinations:

- A history teacher ● a disco dancer ● a sports fanatic
- An elderly man/woman ● a fifteen-year-old person ● a middle aged man

You will have to use the appropriate language and way of speaking for the character you are speaking to.

Alternatively, your teacher might group you according to your original choice of holiday and ask you to keep to your choice.

Role-play the situation. The three characters enter the travel agents' shop. The travel agent has to ask appropriate questions of the characters to sell them a holiday that suits all of them. The three characters will not make it easy to achieve a solution but they must not make it impossible.

Evaluate:

A member of your group should evaluate the travel agents performance. Start by using these prompts. Gain the opinions of all members of the group.

- Was the travel agent listening to the viewpoints of the three characters and thinking at the same time of possible solutions?
- Did the three characters make their preferences and requests clear?
- Were there areas where compromise might have been possible that were identified or missed?

A third person completes an evaluation of the customers' role. Again, collect the opinions of the entire group. Here are some points to get you started.

- How did the characters use different kinds of language to achieve their effect?
- How did the ways the characters behaved help or hinder the exchange?

Review

The final member of each group will feedback the evaluations to the rest of the class. Identify common successful and unsuccessful strategies. Think about how language and attitude can help achieve what you are trying to do. If there is time, your teacher might ask different members of the group to explain whether they were satisfied with what happened and to evaluate the discussion process in which they took part.

You have played a key part in discussion, listening carefully to what you have heard and reporting back on this. You have also used role play to explore a situation.

Making presentations

Aims

- To make a formal presentation, using Standard English and choosing ways of creating an effect on your audience
- To talk about a subject, changing the pace of delivery and tone for a particular effect
- To think about how your strengths in speaking are improving and work out how you can improve them further

Starter session

'Just a minute'

Your teacher will give the class a subject and choose one of you to start. You have to speak on this subject for one minute without repeating yourself and without hesitating. You also have to use grammatically correct English.

The rest of the class must listen very carefully and challenge any speaker who breaks the rules. Language such as "stuff", "sort of", "kind of thing" is **colloquial** and not acceptable in this context. You may repeat words such as "of", "the" and "a/an" but cannot repeat a noun or adjective. Use a stopwatch or a clock with a second hand and time the speaker.

If the speaker is successfully challenged, the challenger takes over the speech with whatever time remains. A successful challenge earns a point. Whoever finishes the speech earns a point.

Subjects might include such topics as 'School sport', 'Boy band', 'Riding a bike'.

Introduction

Successful presentation

It is likely that your 'just a minute' presentations were muddled or disorganised.

Successful presentations are structured so that information or opinions are conveyed clearly and fluently. An audience needs to be interested and entertained or it will not listen and the purpose of the presentation will be lost. Repetition and a lack of structure makes a presentation more difficult to follow. Similarly, if a speaker is not fluent and lapses into slang, the listeners might not follow the point.

A successful structure normally consists of an opening that grabs the audience's attention and encourages them to listen. This might take the form of a question, a short statement or a description of what is happening. This should be followed by the main content, consisting of three or four points that you want to make. Finally, close your presentation so that what you intended to say is clear.

ACTIVITY

You will be given a topic upon which to make a three-minute presentation. The title will correspond to the initial letter of your first name. For example:

Sarah = skiing   Vishali = vegetables   Imran = ice cubes

Tom = trousers   Jason = jet planes   Emma = eggs

Spend five minutes jotting down notes to structure your speech. Jot down a phrase that will help you remember your opening; then think of the points you wish to make, noting them down very briefly. It is important that you do not write everything out. Finally, think of a suitable ending. Use only one prompt card for your talk.

Opening	
Points	1
	2
	3
	4
	5
Conclusion	

Get into groups of four.

Deliver your presentations one at a time to the class. The listeners should not interrupt but should be identifying the strengths and weaknesses of the presentation. When each speaker has finished, complete a table such as the one below:

Speaker: Sarah   **Title of presentation:** Skiing

Section	Point	Timing
Opening	Sport, two planks of wood a hill and snow	1 minute
Points	Bad points: Is dangerous, expensive, often cold is hard work and often looks silly Good points: Great fun, keeps you fit, healthy	1.5 minutes
Conclusion	So popular, people must want to go again.	0.5 minute

Strengths	Weaknesses
Easy to follow with clear points	Not particularly original
Humorous beginning	Ending a little weak
Language formal but friendly	Links between points not clear
Good vocabulary and fluent style	

Review

Choose one speech from your group to present to the whole class. Another member of the group will introduce the speaker and the speech and explain why this particular speech was chosen.

You have thought about how to organise your ideas in giving a presentation, using Standard English and how to deliver this so that it creates an impact on your listeners.

Further developments ▷

Your teacher might decide to ask you to work on your presentation and spend time planning a longer version. You might be asked to bring in presentational devices, such as visual aids, accessories etc.

Language in role

Aims

- To work together to create a character through dramatic methods
- To think about the part you play in a dramatic presentation and how you could improve on this
- To think about how your strengths in speaking are improving and what you need to do to improve further

Starter session

Register volleyball

The class will be divided into two sections. One section will create a list of job titles. For example:

doctor

teacher

traffic warden

shop assistant.

The other section will think of phrases that might be used by people in certain roles. For example, "Get out your homework diaries", might be a common command used by a teacher which would be totally inappropriate for a person doing another job.

Your teacher might subdivide the sections into smaller groups.

The first group will give a job title. The second group will respond by giving a phrase or sentence that can be identified as belonging to the role. Then the second group will give a phrase etc for which the first group will identify a social role.

As a class, decide what you have discovered from this activity. How far did you find that your ideas gave rise to stereotypes?

Introduction

Language in role

People in different roles use language differently. Words and sentences are chosen and structured in a way that fits the purpose, situation and role of the speaker. Sometimes, this is so well known that it becomes stereotyped and is often used in situation comedies.

An example of this is the policeman:

"ello, 'ello, 'ello. What have we got here then?"

This is a comic representation of police language even though very few members of the police would actually say it. Police use of language, or **register**, is more likely to be:

"We were proceeding along North Street in a southerly direction when we noticed a young white male loitering outside the amusement arcade..."

Think about certain social and work groups that might use a specific register or form of language. How many different types can you identify?

You will work in groups of three. Your teacher will allocate a job or social role to each of you. You will also be given a situation. You will be asked to improvise a conversation in which all three take part, using the language that is most appropriate for them.

Examples of this might include:

Participants	Context
Doctor, parking attendant, elderly gentleman	in a car park in the rain
Teacher, parent, child	parents' evening
Shopkeeper, policeman, small child	in a sweet shop

Your **improvisation** should only take five minutes. Once you have reached the time limit, discuss as a group how you each used language. How far did you create your character by their use of language?

Review

Your teacher will ask some of you to perform your improvisations in front of the whole class. You will not tell them who you are. When you have finished, the rest of the class will discuss how you used language and how that described and identified your character. How successful were they in identifying you?

You have thought about how we can gain a sense of what a character is like through the language they use. You have also thought about how to present a character dramatically and the language skills you use to do this.

Further developments ▶

Radio drama could be taped and brought into the class and fragments played to the class. As an alternative starter activity, the class is asked to identify the roles and identities of the speakers and explain how their language places them in a social role.

Agreeing to disagree

Aims

- To listen and pay careful attention to what you need to find out
- To ask questions to make your understanding clearer and to help you think through your ideas
- To think about the different ways information can be put across, such as tone of voice and emphasis
- To use talk to investigate ideas

Starter session

Your teacher will go round the class asking you to identify something you like very much and something that you dislike in the following categories:

sport

fruit

pop groups/bands

vegetables

TV programmes

sport celebrities

colours

film stars

You will be asked to explain your preferences and how strongly you feel.

Introduction

Expressing different opinions

Discussion is often used to achieve an agreement between two different opinions. There are times when no agreement can be reached. If your friends hate carrots, it will be very difficult to persuade them to change their minds, even if it is your preferred food. When exchanging views, we use certain phrases that accept that the other person speaking might be right, even while we feel we are right to hold our point of view too. Examples of these phrases are:

"I can *see* your view but..."

"I understand what you are saying and..."

We can add certain words to our speech that make a difference of opinion less difficult to sort out. Such words appear to agree with or accept the other speaker's view; for example,

"Absolutely..."

"Of course..."

"Certainly..."

Identify these words and phrases as a class. Your teacher will write them on the board.

You will be paired with someone who likes what you dislike or dislikes what you like. For five minutes, discuss your differences. In your conversation you should try to ensure that you do the following:

- Accept that your partner has the right to their opinion
- Keep the conversation pleasant and non-aggressive
- Use as many of the phrases and words that you have identified as helping to acknowledge each other's opinions

Feedback to the rest of the class.
Your teacher might ask you to swap pairs and try another conversation. Compare the experience. Were you better at acknowledging the other person's viewpoint and evaluating how you managed any possible argument?

Review

Your teacher will ask each of you to identify one strategy that your partner used in the conversation that was effective. As a class, can you identify any patterns emerging that were common in successful conversations?

You have thought about how to hold a conversation with someone whose views are different from your own and how to listen carefully to what they have to say. You have considered what are the best questions to ask to find out what they think and, also, how to put your own point of view across effectively.

Persuasive talking

Aims

- To think about how you use language and what you could do to improve your skills
- To change the tone of your delivery in asking questions, for a particular effect
- When listening, to pay careful attention in order to identify what you need to pick out
- To think about all the different ways in which information can be put across, such as tone and emphasis
- To explore issues and relationships through working in role, developing dramatic techniques to do this

Starter session

Your teacher will write on the board: 'I want someone to give me a lift to...'

Think of the different contexts that this might fit. Your teacher will go round the class and brainstorm with you the various situations in which this might occur.

For example, you might be asking a parent or relative for a lift or you could be asking a cab driver. You could be a criminal out of a TV series using threats. How many situations can the class identify?

Once you have finished, your teacher will ask some of you to ask for the lift, using the tone, vocabulary and style that will suit that context. Work in pairs and try using both appropriate and 'inappropriate' language when making your request. For example, what would be the reaction of your friend's parents if you demanded, "Take me to the swimming pool. Now!"

Discuss why language is used differently in different contexts. Identify why some ways of asking are more successful than others.

Feed your conclusions back to the whole class. Your teacher might ask some of you to show the rest of the class your successful or unsuccessful attempts.

Introduction

Politeness and courtesy

The way a request is made and the language used makes a difference between achieving and not achieving your goals. Although polite requests usually work best, if you are polite with your dog, you are unlikely to train him effectively. Although there are occasions when you have to be assertive, authoritative and issue orders, most requests are successful when made with courtesy and politeness.

ACTIVITY

Think of the effect of phrases such as 'Would you mind...?' 'Is it possible...?' 'It would be really nice if...'

As a class, think of as many of these 'polite' phrases as possible. Your teacher will write them on the board.

Work in groups of three. One of you will be asking for something from another member of the group. You will make your request using two different styles of language, one of which will include one or more of the 'polite' phrases. The third member will listen carefully, making notes of the features of the language used and the success of each in achieving the objective. The listener will also make a note of how much time it took for the conversation to come to an end. Now swap around so that each member of the group has the opportunity to make the request, either grant or deny it and take notes.

At the end of each conversation, each member of the group should describe how they felt when making/receiving/observing the request. It might be that the request was denied because the person could not help, but felt guilty or sad as a result. Discuss what it was about the way the request was made that created this effect.

You will try this activity out at least three times.

Review

Your teacher may ask some of you to repeat your role-play and ask the class to evaluate why it was successful or unsuccessful. You will explore the use of 'polite' phrases and decide when they are appropriate. You may be asked to reflect on other occasions when your own language might have helped or hinder you achieving your objective.

The balloon debate

Aims

- To make a formal presentation, using language devices to create a particular effect on your audience
- To use talk to investigate and explore complex issues and ideas
- To play a part in group discussion, moving ideas forward and reporting back on the main points that come up

Starter session

My hero

Your teacher will give you a few minutes to think and then ask each of you to nominate an historical or **contemporary** character who you think made a big impact on or contribution to the world. This could be a scientist, a politician, an heroic person or even an entertainer. It could also be someone unknown to everyone else, such as one of your grandparents whom you admire.

As well as identifying that person, you will be asked to make a very short statement explaining your reasons for nominating your 'hero/heroine'. Listen carefully to the reasons given by the rest of the class and think about which are most convincing.

When you make your own presentation, think of the words and phrases you need to use to get your audience to agree with what you are saying.

> I think David Beckam is an inspiration to young people.

> My grandma is always working for charities and she makes me very proud.

> Our English teacher, Mr McLean, inspires us to enjoy learning every day.

Introduction

Promoting characters

Convincing people of the value of your argument is achieved by using language effectively.

Think about what kind of language would convince your teacher that you were hard working, conscientious and organised, even if you knew that this did not describe you. Give evidence for what you say. Which of the following two examples is most effective?

> 'When have I ever missed a deadline Miss?'

> 'I've never missed a deadline Miss!'

You will also need to adopt a certain manner that makes your listener believe you without making it sound as though you are putting on an act. Sometimes, it is more effective if someone else says what is good about you. When you make your own presentation, think of the words and phrases you need to get your audience to agree with what you are saying.

When putting across your argument, you will need to learn to use what we call **rhetorical devices**. These are phrases used in formal speaking that convince an audience of your belief in what you are saying.

Rhetorical devices can take very different forms. These include:

- Forms of address – using complimentary or formal terms when addressing your audience. For example 'my fellow classmates' or 'ladies and gentlemen'.
- Answering your own questions – developing an argument by putting questions and then answering them, for example 'so what is the answer? The answer is yes.' or 'was that the intention? No it was not.'
- Quoting another speaker – using the words of another speaker, or of someone else, which support your argument, for example 'when my teacher, Mr Jones, said I was hard-working, he was being very kind' or 'Did our own head teacher not tell us of the importance of hard work and concentration?'

You will need to practice using these rhetorical devices in your own formal speaking. Listen very carefully to how experienced public speakers – politicians, journalists, teachers – weave these devices into their speech and learn from them.

Work in groups of six.

Go back to the list of characters you all described in the Starter session at the beginning of the unit.

Discuss the value of the characters you each identified. You have to reduce the number to three. To help you make the decision and focus your discussion, complete this table:

Character	Good points	Bad points
William Shakespeare	Wrote some plays Is important in English Literature	We are tested on them
David Beckham	Plays good football Is a good role model	I don't like football Hasn't saved the world

You have ten minutes to decide which five characters you will get rid of and which you will keep.

In order to persuade your listeners of the importance of your character, you will have to do the following:

- Justify the importance of the character
- Explain how the world would be a better place if the character were retained
- Work on the emotions and sympathy of the group
- Use a manner that encourages the others to want to agree with you.

When you have finished you will tell your teacher and nominate a member to speak to the whole class on behalf of the group.

Try and use some of the rheotorical devices described in the introduction when making your presentation.

Decide amongst you who will take the part of the character and who will act as the **proposer**. The proposer will outline the reasons why this character is valuable. As a group, prepare some prompt cards to help the chosen student make an opening speech.

Your teacher will ask the students playing the characters to come to the front of the class. They are now in an air balloon that is rapidly losing height over the sea. In order to keep the balloon in the air, one person has to be thrown overboard.

The proposer from each group explains to the rest of the class why their character should not be thrown overboard. After these speeches are finished, the rest of the class can ask questions of each character. A vote will be taken and in the event of a tie, the teacher will have the casting vote.

As the balloon is still too heavy, another person has to be thrown overboard. Follow the same procedure but allocate new proposers or your teacher will ask the characters themselves to justify why they should stay on board. Repeat the process until you have one person left in the balloon. Your teacher may decide to throw two people overboard at once, or do it one at a time.

The last character remaining must thank the rest of the class for the support given.

Review

Think about how the decision was made. Discuss how the use of proposals, questions and justifying statements to the audience helped a character stay on board. Identify whether any change of language, style or manner in the way the character was presented could have helped a character who was thrown overboard remain on the balloon.

Selling your ideas

Aims

- To give an explanation of your ideas, linking these to an image or diagram
- To listen carefully, identifying what information you need to pick out and what questions you need to ask
- To play an effective part in discussion, recognising and building on other people's contributions
- To think about how your strengths in speaking are improving, working out what you need to do to improve further

Starter session

Work in pairs. Find an object in the classroom or in your bag that is not valuable. This could be a stick of chalk, a single shoe or even an empty crisp packet. 'Sell' the object to your partner. You might like to think about how you might convince your partner by:

- Finding a good use for the object
- Exaggerating its value
- Explaining that it's fashionable

Change places. Discuss what techniques you used and whether they were successful. Change partners and try again.

Introduction

Persuasive talking

Persuasive language is used to sell an idea or a product. To do this, you have to be able to identify the good points – the benefits or worth – of what you are selling. Some salespeople are so successful in using language that they often sell to people who did not want or need the product. Think about how this is achieved.

On a piece of paper, write down an idea for one of the following:

- A new invention
- A new television programme
- A new board or computer game
- A new school rule or different timetable

Work in groups of four. Your teacher will allocate you a category. Plan a presentation that will 'sell' your idea to another group. On a large sheet of paper, make a sketch/diagram which each person must use as a visual prompt at some point during their presentation. You will take specific roles. For example:

Selling a new television programme

Presenters: Group A	Audience: Group B
Designer: Emma	Executive producer: Imran
Researcher: Joe	Chief Accountant: Kate
Games host: Ayesha	Scheduler: Ben
Director: James	Advertising exec: Tom

Selling an invention

Presenters: Group A	Audience: Group B
Designer: Ben & Tom	Managing Director: Paula
Researcher: Imran	Chief Accountant: Sasha
Technology: Kate	Chief Executive: Priya
	Works Manager: Jo

To make a presentation successfully, groups have to work together knowing exactly which area is their responsibility. You will see from the roles taken by the audience, that each person will have particular areas of concern. The accountant will want to know about profitability, whilst the works manager might be more concerned about how they can make the product.

Each group will make one presentation and act as an audience once.

Review

Each group should evaluate their presentation and how well they performed. Your teacher will also ask you to talk to the class about how another group presented their idea. Evaluate the presentations describing the strengths and weaknesses and whether they were successful in selling their ideas.

The Chat Show

Aims

- To develop interview techniques which include planning a series of linked questions, helping the respondent to give useful answers.
- To use Standard English to explain, explore or justify an idea
- To contribute to the organisation of a group activity

Starter session

As a class brainstorm, list all the television chat shows that you know. Can you place them into categories? Some use ordinary people with interesting stories and some feature celebrities. Your list might start something like this:

Ordinary People	Celebrities
Kilroy	Parkinson

Introduction

Creating a chat show

The chat show is a popular form of entertainment and relies upon conversation to entertain listeners. Some shows are serious and deal with important issues; some are more light-hearted. The job of the chat show host is to get information out of their guests that they believe will interest their audiences. Your teacher may show you some extracts from current shows on television.

Write the name of a 'guest' for a chat show on a piece of paper. The 'guest' should be a public figure and can come from history or be alive today. Give it to your teacher. After shuffling the pieces of paper, your teacher will distribute them. You must keep the name of the guest you are going to portray secret.

Go into groups of three. Identify all the chat show hosts that you know and put them into categories. You should include the following categories:

Male/Female **Personal interests/Public issues**

Serious/Comic

Make a list of what makes a good chat show host.

Discuss how a chat show guest is chosen. List some potential guests that would interest the same audience and some that would not. Plan your chat show, identifying a good chat show host and a selection of guests.

Share your ideas with the rest of the class. You are now going to play out a chat show.

Choose a member of the class or use your teacher to play the chat show host. The chat show host will introduce the show and call in the guests by asking different members of the class to come forward. When your name is called, you assume the identity of the 'guest' who is named on the piece of paper that your teacher gave you earlier. The host will interview you, trying to make you as interesting as possible.

Use language to entertain your audience in an appropriate way that also helps them identify who you are. Your host may decide to bring on another guest to engage in conversation and when you are identified you will be swapped with the person in the class who has guessed your identity.

Review

You have worked together as a group to explore what makes a good chat show and thought carefully about the kinds of questions you need to ask in order to find out the information you need. You have chosen your language to have a particular effect on your audience, using Standard English.

Further developments ▷

You could also devise a chat show involving the characters from a text you are currently studying. This could be a way of helping you explore their role and the way the author has constructed them.

For example, if you are reading George Bernard Shaw's 'Pygmalion', your chatshow might begin like this:

Host: So, Henry Higgins, what was your opinion of Miss Dolittle when you met her for the first time?

Higgins: I saw her as a challenge.

Host: What do you think you achieved in working with her?

Higgins: Well, I'm not sure how she saw it, but ....

Arguing your case

Aims

- To plan a series of questions, in order to find out the information you want
- To compare the different points of view you will hear, identifying the implications and looking for examples of **bias**
- To discuss and consider the truth of the conflicting evidence which will be presented
- To work in role to explore different situations

Starter session

In pairs, think about some incidents which might happen that would need investigation and which could have several points of view. You have five minutes to think about this. Some of them could be linked to trouble at school or more serious issues that involve the wider community. You might like to think about what you might have watched on television that could be used. If you need help in thinking up possible situations, there are some ideas below.

Combine your pairs into groups of four and decide upon which story to use. Is it possible to find more than one version of events in the story

Share your 'case' with the rest of the class. As a class, decide how many versions of this story are possible.

Example 1

A friend said, a little while ago, that you could always borrow her revision notes if you needed them. Your friend was away just before an important test was coming up, but you knew that her notes for that subject were in her unlocked locker. You went to her locker to borrow them, but a teacher saw you...

Example 2

You failed to turn up for an important football match. The team lost, and the coach wants to drop you from the team. You had a good reason but did not tell the coach beforehand...

Introduction

Listening to different arguments

An 'argument' is another word for a discussion but also suggests conflict. One purpose of an argument is to make a convincing case for your point of view. Arguments can involve different points of view but agreements can be reached if the people concerned are prepared to listen as well as to talk.

'Arguing your case' also suggests that there are different possible interpretations of events. This term is often used when a **mediator** is involved who is trying to find out the "truth" of events. This can occur in small incidents such as a difference of opinion as to what happened in the school playground and in more serious issues that might involve the police or magistrates!

In your group of four, work on your existing story. You will work in pairs to begin with, both developing stories that show the other pair to be responsible for the incident you are using. Construct the story that best suits you and devise a list of questions that you can ask the other 'side' that will help you convince other people that your story is the most believable.

Take your story to the rest of the class. One pair goes first, telling the story. The other pair can then ask their questions before they take their turn. The first pair then asks the second pair questions.

The class will vote for the most believable story.

Review

As a class, discuss the following questions:
- Which questions were most useful?
- What other questions could (or should) have been asked?
- How effective was each story in getting the key points across?

You have worked in role to present different versions of events in different situations and, in groups, weighed up what you have heard, deciding on what you think is believable and what is biased.

Further developments ▷

You could play out a court case. Allocate lawyers, witnesses and court officials and prepare a case. Your teacher may decide to do this with characters in the texts you are currently studying.

The Citizenship Foundation organise a Magistrates Competition for lower school students and a Mock Bar Trial for older students. Schools prepare cases and compete against one another in real magistrates and court cases. This can also be useful for work on the citizenship, key skills and personal and social curriculum.

The formal debate

Aims

- To use Standard English to explore and justify an issue
- To express and compare different points of view, identifying the key issues of what you hear and weighing up the conflicting evidence
- To come to a decision about your final viewpoint

Starter session

Remind yourselves of unit 2 when you had to argue a point of view. Think of an issue that would be sufficiently interesting to the whole class. These could be school-related as in:

- Re-organising the school day or terms
- Changes in the canteen or tuck shop

Or could be wider such as:

- Hunting
- Crime and punishment

Your teacher will write your suggestions on the board.

As a class, discuss one of the issues that you would like to focus upon.

Remember that the issue must be one that everyone can contribute to. Avoid anything which could be described as too 'narrow' – that is, addressing an issue of interest to a limited number of people.

Introduction

The debating chamber

Your ideas for discussion will form the basis for a formal debate. Debating is a very structured activity and is used by the Houses of Parliament when deciding law. The place where the debate takes place is called the **debating chamber**.

Like many structured activities, there are names used for the different stages of a debate. This is why the idea must be structured into a proposition or a **motion** and take the form of, "This house believes that ....." It is usual for one person to **propose** the motion and another person to **oppose**. Two other people **second** the motion by speaking in favour and against. A chairperson, called 'the Speaker' in the House of Commons, ensures that procedures are followed and offers everybody present, called 'the floor' to give their opinion, either for or against the motion. The procedure allows different views to be given in an orderly way.

When everyone has spoken or time has run out, the Chairperson asks for a vote. If the vote is in favour of the motion, the chair will say, "The motion that (repeating the proposition) is hereby carried". If the vote is against, the chair will say, "The motion that ..... is hereby defeated."

This flow from proposition to conclusion can be shown in the following chart.

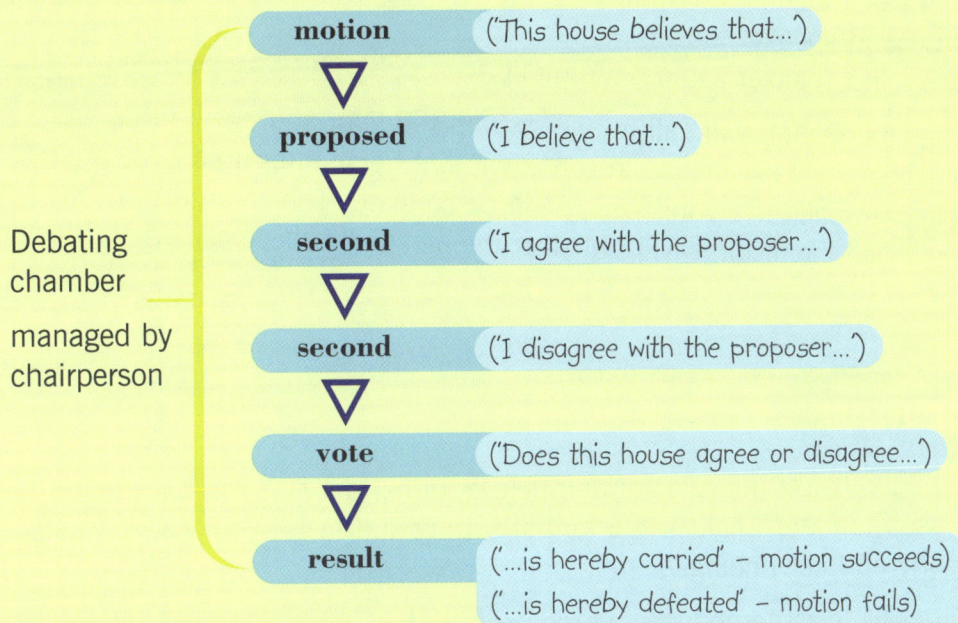

	motion	('This house believes that...')
	▽	
	proposed	('I believe that...')
	▽	
Debating chamber	**second**	('I agree with the proposer...')
	▽	
managed by chairperson	**second**	('I disagree with the proposer...')
	▽	
	vote	('Does this house agree or disagree...')
	▽	
	result	('...is hereby carried' – motion succeeds) ('...is hereby defeated' – motion fails)

Because it is a formal situation, you must use Standard English when you are speaking.

Your teacher will ask you all to think about the issue you have chosen to debate and will ask for your initial opinion. You will then go into groups of four with students who agree with you.

In your groups make a list of all the points that support your opinion. You should think about facts, expert opinion and **anecdotes** (stories) that will help make your viewpoint more convincing. If you have time, can you think of points that your opposition might raise so that you can plan a **response**?

Choose one member of the group and help plan a speech lasting two minutes that will present your viewpoint. You should write down key points on small cards or pieces of paper. Do not write the speech out in full.

You will debate the issue as a whole class. Your teacher will select four speakers from the group representatives to take the roles of:

- Speaker for the motion
- Speaker against the motion
- Second speaker for the motion
- Second speaker against the motion

The chairperson will call for views from the floor and ensure that everybody gets a chance to speak without being interrupted. He or she will then call for a vote, which will be counted. The chairperson will announce the result, saying whether the motion has been carried or defeated.

Review

You have learnt the rules of and held a formal debate. You have learnt how to use Standard English in a formal setting and to get your point across clearly and convincingly.

You need to remember the words used to describe the different stages of a formal debate. In pairs, make a list of the key words and then ask your partner to describe what they mean in less than twenty words. If you can't remember what any of the words mean, go back to the introduction above, or look at your notes from the activity above.

The formal meeting

Aims

- To think about the contributions you will make to a discussion, helping to organise the activity in a structured way
- To consider your ability as a listener and as a speaker, in a different context
- To use Standard English to present your position

Starter session

As a whole class, think of when there are occasions to have meetings. It might be a meeting of the class to organise teams for sports day, or it could be a meeting of the schools council. Societies and clubs have meetings. Make a list of all the kinds of meetings in which you could be involved. Your teacher will write them on the board.

Introduction

A club meeting

Meetings are held to achieve a purpose. This can be to reach a decision or to discuss an issue. The purpose can be seen in the list of things that will be discussed. This is called an **agenda**. In order for them to work well, people must take on different roles.

In a commercial organisation, viewpoints and concerns are linked with the job function. An accountant for example, will primarily be interested in finance whereas a personnel officer will have concerns to do with staffing. For an organisation to function successfully, the views of all key people need to be addressed. To ensure different people are given equal opportunities to get their points across, a meeting needs to be carefully managed.

The following roles are important for a successful meeting:

- A chairperson: who conducts the meeting and ensures everyone contributes
- A secretary: who makes notes of the discussion and of any decisions and also clarifies points for everyone

Meetings are made more successful if everyone listens to each other and encourages everyone to give their views in order to reach a decision.

ACTIVITY

Get into groups of six. Your teacher will give you a name of a club or society. It could be from one of the following:

The young supporters club of your local football team

The committee of the youth club

Or it might be more imaginative such as

Travellers through space society

Skateboarders against grass verges society

You are going to organise and run a meeting. In your group, organise an agenda for a possible meeting. You should start with

- Apologies for absence
- Minutes of the last meeting

You must then list the items for discussion and for which decisions must be made and conclude with:

- Any other business

Your teacher will allocate you a set amount of time in which to conduct your meeting. It may be necessary to reduce your agenda if the time is short. Choose a chairperson and a secretary from your group and agree a role for each of the other members of the group. For example if it is a sports club, one might be the coach, another might be the treasurer; one might be the captain of the team whilst another could be the physiotherapist.

When you have finished, each member of the club who 'attended' the meeting should evaluate their role and their usefulness to the meeting.

Review

Your teacher will ask the secretary of each meeting to give a brief account of what happened in the meeting and the decisions that were taken. Evaluate how many of the meetings were successful. Use the following questions as part of your evaluation:

- Did they finish the agenda in the time allocated?
- Did everyone have the opportunity to make a contribution?
- Did anyone dominate the meeting or make it difficult?
- How could the meeting have been more successful?

It will be difficult to choose a winner, but discuss why some of the meetings were more successful than others and write a list of key points to improve the less successful meetings.

Applications and Interviews

Aims

- To work at developing interview techniques, which include planning a series of questions and helping the person being interviewed to give useful answers
- To compare the different points of view expressed by others in your group
- To extend the skills you are developing in drama, working in role to explore issues.
- To think about your ability as a speaker, on your own and in discussion, considering how to improve on this

Starter session

Think of the times when you have been or could be interviewed. With the help of your teacher, make a list and write them on the board.

Go into pairs. Your teacher will tell you what the interview will be. It could be an interview to get into the school, an interview for a paper round or babysitting.

Act out an interview and take turns in being the interviewer.

Evaluate whether you performed well in both roles. Remember, the interviewer is looking for information. Did the applicant achieve what s/he wanted? What could have been done better?

Interview topic	Acted out by	Evaluation
To get a paper round	James and Lauren	Information put across in a convincing manner
To get into a new school		

Introduction

Going for interview

An interview is a specific form of meeting and is also designed to help people to share information and make decisions. It is important that the interviewer obtains the information that is wanted from the interviewee.

The information will be different depending upon the purpose of the interview. If it is a job interview, the interviewer will have a job description and probably a description that best fits the most suitable applicant. The applicant will need to convince the interviewer that s/he is that applicant.

As with any meeting, an interview has an 'agenda' – a purpose. Different people in the interview may have different agendas, different purposes and needs. Identifying what that is can often help create a successful interview.

Presentation is very important and using the most appropriate language is essential if applicants are going to achieve their goals. Remember you should always use Standard English in this kind of situation.

ACTIVITY

You will be organised into groups of three or four and will conduct a 'GCSE Options' interview. As a class, discuss the various 'agendas' the following participants might hold: teachers, pupil, parents.

Make a list of all the possible 'agendas' as below:

Pupil	Parent	Teacher
Wants to do the same subjects as friend to be in the same class	Want her to do languages so we can travel abroad	Don't take my subject!

Organise your group into pupil, parent(s) and teacher. Your teacher may give you an 'agenda' or leave you to invent your own. Your task, as a group, is to conduct an options interview. Each of you will want a specific result. The national curriculum only gives you a choice of subjects in humanities, languages, technology and arts but your teacher may decide to suspend it for the purpose of this task.

The interview might begin something like this:

Form teacher: So, Vanisha, have decided what you want to do for your GCSE subjects?

Vanisha: I really like Art, but I'm not sure whether to do Graphics.

Parent: We want her to study subjects that will be helpful to her later...

After the interview which can only last ten minutes, share your agendas and evaluate your success. Discuss how a better result could have been achieved.

Review

Report back to the whole class whether you achieved your objective. Your teacher will help you to draw up a list of strategies and tactics that help an interview work well for you.

You have worked together as a group, using role-play to explore different points of view. You have thought about the way linked questions can achieve a particular purpose. You have thought about how to use language effectively.

Monologues in role

Aims

- To identify the underlying implications raised by a reading, looking beneath the surface at what is being said
- To identify the skills and techniques you are developing through drama, reflecting on your skills as a speaker

Starter session

In pairs, construct some characters by filling in a table such as the one started below:

Gender	Age	Occupation	Nationality
Female	14	Student at school	British (English)
Male	67	Retired bus driver	British (Scottish)

Try speaking a few sentences as if you are that character. Without describing yourself give clues from what you say about your age, gender and situation. How quickly can your partner guess which one on the list you are playing?

Introduction

Performing a monologue

A monologue is a piece of drama spoken and performed by a single actor. Your teacher might read some extracts of well-known monologues to you. They are long speeches, uninterrupted by dialogue. When we listen to them, we get an idea of the character of the speaker. We often use monologues in real life when we reflect upon experiences and feelings. Your teacher might show you some extracts from videos such as Alan Bennett's *Talking Heads*.

In this activity, you will be constructing monologues.

You can either create a character by using the table which you completed in your paired activity or use an existing one. This could be a famous character from history or from modern times or it could be a fictional character from a current soap opera. You might like to base it around someone you know. Usually the monologue centres around a memory of an incident or an anecdote but as the character speaks, further information is revealed.

Work in pairs to help each other devise a monologue. Discuss which characterisation would be appropriate for you and what would make a suitable focus for the monologue. How would you weave in information about the character in a way that would not be too artificial?

Practise your monologues to each other.

Review

Your teacher may ask some of you to perform your monologues in front of the class.

When you have finished, reflect on the differences between practising in front of your partner and performing in front of a larger audience. Is it more off-putting when you are speaking to more people? Consider the differences between working with other people when you perform for an audience and your solo activity. Were you more nervous on your own? Is it easier when you are not relying on other people?

You have worked at producing a monologue, thinking about how you can show a character's thoughts and feelings through what is said and what is left out. You have thought about your skills in dramatic techniques and your abilities as a speaker.

Please note
Your teacher may set this piece for a speaking and listening assessment for the end of your Key Stage Three course.

Using language for effect

Aims

- To use a drama technique **working in role** to explore issues; you will work at developing this skill
- To think about how to develop and improve your ability as a speaker

Starter session

In groups of four, think of some situations where you use language to help someone cope. This could be a friend who has failed an examination, two fellow students who are having an argument or someone who is panicking because they have lost their mobile phone. You may need to be encouraging and motivating. Discuss what kind of 'attitude' you would have to take to help them.

Write down the situations on a piece of paper and hand them to your teacher. Discuss, as a class, what kind of attitude is best to use in these situations.

Introduction

Working in role

Choosing the right language and the right way of speaking to someone when they are either stressed or hyperactive is vital. The wrong word or an inappropriate tone can stop communication and create the opposite effect to the one you hoped to achieve.

Certain phrases such as, "I am sorry you feel…" can help and encouraging people to talk about their feelings with "Tell me what's wrong …" can begin to calm someone because they often just want someone to listen to their complaint. In this task, you will role-play some of the situations you identified and use different language and tones to see which one is best to use.

You will work in pairs and threes acting out some of the situations you have identified. Your teacher will give you the situation. They will involve some of the following:

- Calming someone
- Motivating someone to work or play hard
- Encouraging someone to try something again after they have not succeeded
- Cheering up a friend
- Helping to resolve an argument
- Dealing with a complaint or an angry person

Act out the situation, taking it in turns. Try the same situation, using different types of language and attitudes. Discuss and evaluate which was the most successful way of dealing with the situation.

Review

Your teacher will ask some of you to act out your situations in front of the class. Some of you may be given the same situation so that the class can evaluate which is the best way of dealing with it. List, as a class, which were the most helpful expressions in doing this. Were there any which were unhelpful? If so, why was this?

You have explored different situations and the way language can be used in these, working in role. You have thought about how to improve your abilities in speaking.

Using the language of the media [1]

Aims

- To compare different points of view, thinking about differences and similarities
- To discuss the evidence for these points of view and try to reach an agreement
- To aim to work effectively as a group in doing this

Starter session

In groups of four, make a list of non-fiction programmes that you know in the media: Identify them in categories such as the table below:

News	Sports reporting	Documentary
News at 10	Match of the Day	Panorama

Choose one programme from each of the sections and choose a topic that would be associated with it. For example, if the three above were used you could choose

Bulletin about factory closure   **Report of Arsenal v Man Utd**

Crime Report

Discuss how these programmes might use language to tell their audiences about the events.

Introduction

Media language

The media use very specific language that accurately targets their audiences. Look at the differences between the types of news programmes that you might know. For example, News at 10 is far more formal than the news bulletins on daytime TV which are still more formal than any news item given on breakfast TV. Your teacher may have a selection of clips to show you the differences.

Compare the way a newsreader delivers the news from that found in a daily newspaper. Oral language, however formal, is still very different from written. It is important that items are timed very carefully not only because audiences want to receive information quickly, but because of the careful planning of programmes. Notice how interviewers extract information and quickly stop the activity when time is short. Some of the best news journalism can be found on BBC radio and your teacher may play you taped extracts.

ACTIVITY

You will work in groups of four for this activity. Look at the following news headlines:

LARGE FACTORY CLOSES AND THOUSANDS MADE REDUNDANT

NEW STAR TAKES FIVE AWARDS AT THE BRITS

Top politician accused of taking bribes

Donna Spinner scores winning goal in Ladies Hockey tournament

Famous film star moves to Britain

Drowning dog is saved by heroic fireman

England, Scotland, Wales and Ireland all in the world cup

Earthquake in Pacific island devastates area

In your groups, discuss:

- which is the most important news item if this was the content of the evening news?
- what factors make news important?

- if you were presenting the news, discuss how you would deliver these items. You will need to think about tone, register of language, attitude and body language, which piece of news it will follow etc.

Divide into two pairs. One pair will look at these news items and list them in order of importance for News at 10. The other pair will do the same but for GMTV. [Your teacher may give you alternatives] You may leave out items if you wish but you must consider why the editors for those programmes would choose to do so.

Review

Your teacher will ask each group to explain their choice and the order in which they placed the news bulletins. As well as matching the item with the audience of the programme, you will need to explain how the "seriousness" of the issue helps place them in an order of importance and describe how you would present the programme. The class will discuss the different conclusions and your teacher will summarise the key points that have come up from discussion.

You have worked together effectively as a group in comparing the relative place of items in a news programme. You have also thought about the appropriate language and manner to use in presenting the different items.

Using the language of the media [2]

Aims

- To contribute to the organisation of a group activity in structuring ideas and solving problems, looking at different alternatives
- To consider how you could improve your ability as a speaker
- To think about when it is necessary to use Standard English

Starter session

What makes news? As a class, list some incidents that would prove interesting to listeners of a local radio station. You might like to think in the following categories:

- National interest
- Local interest only
- Sports reports
- Humorous incidents
- Accidents and tragedies
- Scandal
- Information for the reader (weather, TV listings etc)

Here is the Six O' Clock News...

Go into pairs: either using some of the ideas brought up in class or your own knowledge and imagination, construct a brief storyline for each of the categories. You do not have to write it all down, just make brief notes to help you remember.

Introduction

Radio news

Language and how it is used is particularly important for radio news as there is no opportunity to show pictures as there is in television. Just as there are different audiences and interests for television, so there is for radio. Compare the news bulletins on music stations with talk radio. Your teacher may have some extracts for you to listen to.

Mood, tone and vocabulary are vital for the radio news reader and journalist because there is no opportunity to show attitude through body language. In the following activity, you are going to devise your own short news programme for the radio. It could be for local or national radio.

ACTIVITY

As a class, share out your ideas from the starter session above. Decide amongst you which are the best storylines. Discuss what makes a good storyline and evaluate how you made your decision.

The class will be divided into two large groups. One group will organise a 10-15 minute news programme for one audience and the other group will do the same for a different audience. Your teacher will select the audience and the radio station for you.

In your large groups quickly organise yourself into the following:

- General editor and assistant.
- Groups of 2/3 who will each work on a news item from one of the categories.

Your editor will chair a group meeting that will decide the following issues:

- the tone of each piece
- the treatment of the storyline; this might be the one you agreed in class or an alternative one. Your teacher might have already made this decision.
- how long each story will be

You will have ten minutes to make notes on your story and prepare the item. This could be a news reporter merely stating the facts or it could take the form of an interview with someone at the scene, or the football manager etc. While you are doing this, the editor and assistant will decide the order of the stories that the news programme will include.

Go back into your large group to receive instructions from the editor as to the order of the programme. Your editor may wish to hear your ideas, but finally s/he has the decision to make.

You may be asked to tape your programme for playback to the class or do it "live" in front of an audience.

Review

Your teacher will ask you to reflect on the experience and discuss the issues surrounding the way news is presented. Each group will briefly summarise their discussion and explain their decisions about how they would treat the stories. The editor and assistant will explain why they wanted a particular tone and why they included or excluded certain news items.

As a class, discuss what you have learned about using language in this context: when you needed to use more formal Standard English, when it was appropriate to be more relaxed, when you tried to make it sound more exciting, when you tried to be factual.

If you do have the opportunity to hear the news programmes, each group should evaluate the success of the other in achieving their aims and objectives.

You have worked together as a group, weighing up different possibilities and aiming to come to an agreement. You have considered the kind of language, such as Standard English, it is appropriate to use in presenting different kinds of information.

Public speaking [1]

Aims

- To develop your skills as a speaker in a different kind of context
- To think about how you could improve on these
- To use Standard English to explore and expand on a subject

Starter session

Think of occasions when someone makes a speech. There will be formal occasions such as speech day and weddings. You would have seen some on television in award ceremonies. There are also less formal occasions when you are celebrating a birthday or a coach speaking to a sports team. The class will brainstorm these and your teacher will write them on the board. You may wish to place them in Formal and Informal categories. Make a list of people who may be called upon to make a speech and place them in Formal and Informal categories. For example:

Formal	Speakers	Informal	Speakers
Wedding receptions	Bridegroom/Parent	Birthday meal	Parents
Speech Day	Visiting speaker	Family celebration	Family

Introduction

Making a speech

Although public speaking seems rather old fashioned, there are occasions when you have to speak in front of an audience to thank someone or to make a little speech. It is still usual for speeches to be given at wedding receptions and they follow a set format. You may have had guest speakers at prize giving or speech day at school.

For formal occasions, where a guest speaker is addressing an audience, it is usual for someone to introduce them, explaining who they are and why they are speaking. After the guest speaker has made their speech, a third person usually thanks them. Although the first speaker can prepare a speech from the information they have been given, the third person has to listen very carefully to the main speech in order that they can refer to some of the points made. Remember that in formal situations, you should use Standard English.

ACTIVITY **A**

Two minute autobiographies

You will work in pairs for this activity. Spend five minutes on this. You will interview each other and find out some interesting biographical material. You can either be yourself or adopt another character. Your task is to jot down brief notes on your partner that will help you tell someone else about them. Think of an angle; is there something amusing or heroic upon which you could base your brief description? Now move into different pairs and give a little speech to each other that describes the first partner. Evaluate your performances. Were they interesting?

You will work in groups of three. From the list that you identified, you or your teacher will allocate some situations and some speakers. Discuss whether the situation is formal or informal and decide who the audience would be. Your task is to make a two minute speech of introduction. This should consist of:

- A brief but interesting biography of the speaker
- What they are currently doing
- The subject of their speech.

Take it in turns to prepare an introduction to a speaker in both formal and informal situations.

Review

Your teacher will ask each of you to deliver your introductory speeches. After each speech, the class will guess what the situation and context is and consider how interested they would be in listening to the speaker once they heard the introduction. (You can deliberately make them sound boring if your teacher thinks it would make it more amusing!)

Evaluate what makes an introductory speech interesting and promotes interest in the person who will be speaking.

You have practised speaking in a different, more formal context and also used Standard English to do so. You have thought about how effective you are in doing this.

Public Speaking [2]

Aims

- To use Standard English to make a presentation
- To think about your abilities as a speaker in a different, more formal, situation and how you could improve on these.

Starter session

As a class think of some ideas that could be turned into a speech lasting five minutes. With the help of your teacher construct a table that categorises them as follows:

Occasions	Celebrations	Awards ceremonies	Gatherings
Wedding	Christmas	The Oscars	Sports Club
Barmitzva	Eid	Speech Day	Leavers Ball

Remind yourselves of the kind of speeches that would be given at these occasions.

Introduction

Speaking at public occasions

We can divide public speaking into two further types other than formal and informal. One kind of speech is directed by its occasion. For example, in a Western wedding reception, it is usual for the Father of the bride to make a speech about his daughter and his prospective son-in-law. At a Bharat Natyam (Hindu Temple ceremony) the Guest of Honour makes a more general speech although it is important to refer to the girl who is dancing.

There are also occasions when the subject matter is less determined by the event. This kind of speech could be performed at a Public Speaking Competition or at a formal dinner where well-known figures are asked to attend and make an entertaining speech. The second type of speech is more likely to have an introductory speech and a vote of thanks. Because these are formal occasions, Standard English should always be used.

ACTIVITY **A**

As a class brainstorm a list of topics that could be used to entertain an audience. This could be based on a proverb, such as:

- Charity begins at home
- Absence makes the heart grow fonder

or it could be on an issue such as:

- The 21st century will show the superiority of the female gender
- A rally for males to regain lost ground

You will work in groups of three to provide three speeches to entertain an audience. The introduction will be given in two minutes, the main speech must take no longer than seven minutes and no shorter than five. The vote of thanks should last 2 minutes. You may use prompt cards to help you but you are not allowed to read your speeches.

Introducing a speaker

Find out some background information about the speaker. The name, present position and what they do should be mentioned. Reference to his authority to address the audience should be made. The tone should be appreciative that this speaker has agreed to make the speech and a suitable atmosphere should be created. You need to be short and focused. When you are addressing your audience, you should also direct their attention to the speaker.

Vote of thanks

The person giving this must listen very carefully to the main speaker. Sum up on behalf of the audience the enjoyment and benefits that you received from the talk. Be cheerful but not too casual. Look at the speaker when you give your thanks and use the name at least in the first and final sentences.

Go into groups of three and plan a speech that is suitable for either an informal occasion or a celebration, such as a wedding, a family gathering or a social occasion when you want to address the people present.

Plan out a speech and deliver it to each other. Discuss the importance of tone, audience and mood in constructing your speech.

Review

Your teacher may ask some of you to give your speeches to the rest of the class who will decide how interesting they were. You are not allowed to use notes and, if you use prompt cards, you must not rely on them too much.

You have worked at introducing a speaker and making a formal speech. You have thought about how to improve your speaking skills and what you need to do to become more effective. You have practised using Standard English in an appropriate situation.

Performing scenes from a play

Aims

- To develop and compare different interpretations of a scene by Shakespeare or another dramatist
- To think about how to convey action, character, atmosphere and tension
- To extend the skills you are developing in drama
- To be ready to write an evaluation of what you have done

Starter session

In groups of four, list all the plays you can think of that you've seen or read since you've been in Year 9. Now brainstorm what the difference is between reading a play and seeing it on stage, or a film or television version. Your teacher will collect your ideas as you feed them back to the class.

Introduction

Creating a performance

You have probably read several plays since you've been in secondary school and, now you're in year 9, you will certainly be reading a play by Shakespeare. You are going to look now at bringing a particular scene to life.

Get in groups of between four and six. Choose a short scene or part of a longer scene from the play you are looking at in class – try to choose one that has fewer main characters than you have in your group.

Think of where the action is taking place – you might want to give it a modern setting.

For each main character, discuss and note down
- how s/he would be feeling at that point in the play
- what s/he would be thinking
- how s/he would be speaking – angrily, nervously, calmly etc
- how the character would behave towards other characters at that point in the play
- what s/he would be wearing

What are the key moments of tension in this scene? What are the most dramatic moments? Are there any changes in mood?

Allocate the parts and choose one of your group to be director.

Prepare a performance of the scene: you don't need to learn your lines but make sure you are very familiar with what you have to say.

If you can, include some of the original language of the play, especially where you feel words or phrases are particularly important.

The director should think about where characters are standing, how they are moving, how slowly or quickly they should speak, how the atmosphere should be conveyed.

Once your performances are ready, either have one group show another group what they have prepared, or your teacher may ask each group to act out the scene in front of the class.

Review

In your groups, discuss what you felt was successful about your performance and what made it so. Was there anything you were less happy with? What could have been done differently to improve it? Try to think of specific points that would have made a difference.

As a class, discuss the various impressions and interpretations that were created in the different performances. Were there any common features? Were there any unusual features? What worked best?

You have worked together to present a performance of a scene from a play, considering how to convey the effects you think the playwright intended. You have used your dramatic techniques to explore character, mood and action.

Further developments ▷

Your teacher may ask you to write a **critical evaluation** of what you have done and the ideas that were behind your performance.

Glossary

Word	Unit	Page	Definition and example
Agenda	9/4	81	A list of points that need to be covered in a meeting. *"The Chairman handed out the agenda to the people attending the meeting before it started."*
Anecdote	9/3	80	An account of something that has actually happened to you. *"I used the anecdote about what happened to my dog to show what I meant about keeping pets."*
Argument	7/9a	36	What you think in a discussion. *"My argument is that smoking is bad for your health."*
Atmosphere/ Mood	7/3	13	The feeling you want to create in a story or description. *"In my writing, I tried to conjure up an atmosphere of mystery and gloomy mood."*
Audience	8/1	44	The person or people who will be listening to what you are saying. *"My audience for what I had to say was my closest friend."*
Bias	9/2	75	Presenting one point of view more strongly than another. *"She was very biased in her account of what happened."*
Book review	7/2	10	An account of what a book is about, the way it is written and how enjoyable it is. *"In my book review, I am going to tell you about the storyline, the characters and what I thought about it."*
Brainstorm	7/8a	28	To jot down as many words or ideas as you can think of in a short time. *"Our group brainstormed all the things we could think of in connection with the topic."*
Caricature	7/4	17	A version of a character that is exaggerated, so that it is rather ridiculous. *"When I played the part of an angry mother, I didn't think carefully enough about she would really be like: it turned into a caricature."*
Colloquial	8/5	55	Chatty. For example: *"I was sort of thinking what I was gonna do."*

Word	Unit	Page	Definition and example
Compromise	8/3	49	Agreement. *"We reached a compromise, even though we had disagreed to begin with."*
Contemporary	8/9	66	Of the present day, of the same time. *"Tony Blair is a contemporary politician; he is Prime Minister at the moment."*
Critical evaluation	9/10	106	A detailed and thoughtful analysis of how successful you have been with a piece of work.
Debate	7/9b	38	A formal discussion; to discuss formally. *"We held a debate about whether animals should be used in testing different products."*
Debating chamber	9/3	78	The place where a debate takes place.
Develop their vocabulary	7/8a	30	Broaden the range of words used. *"Reading a wider range of books will help you develop your vocabulary."*
Dialogue	7/1	8	Conversation between two or more people. *"I included dialogue between two of the characters in my story, to make it more interesting."*
Dilemma	7/6	23	A situation where it is difficult to find a solution to a problem. *"Whether to tell my friend what I had heard was a dilemma."*
Evaluate	7/1	8	To decide on how successful or effective something has been. *"We evaluated whether our discussion went well."*
Imperatives	7/8a	28	Orders. *"I used a series of imperatives in describing how to play the game."*
Improvisation	8/6	60	A scene or piece of dialogue which is made up on the spur of the moment, not prepared.
Location	7/8a	30	Place. *"The location I am in now is the classroom."*
Mediator	9/2	76	The person who helps two or more people to come to an agreement. *"The teacher acted as mediator to try and sort out the argument in class."*
Motion	9/3	79	The subject to be tested in a debate.
Narrative	7/1	6	A story; story-telling. *"In this narrative, I will be telling you about …"*

Word	Unit	Page	Definition and example
Narrator	7/1	8	The person telling the story. *"The narrator of my story is the girl who makes the discovery about …"*
Negotiate	8/3	49	Try to reach an agreement. *"We negotiated the time we would meet."*
Oral	8/3	51	Spoken. *"My oral diary was told to the rest of the group."*
Pace	7/1	6	Measure of speed. *"This story moves at a fast pace."*
Perspective	8/2	46	Viewpoint. *"Your perspective will depend on how you see the situation, the part you played in it."*
Persuasion	7/9a	36	Attempting to change someone's mind. *"I used persuasion to change her position."*
Point of view	7/9a	36	Your opinion on a subject. *"Clare had a different point of view from Helen."*
Prepositions	7/8a	30	A 'placing' word which shows the relationship between a noun or pronoun and the rest of the sentence. *"Drive across the crossroads, go along the road and turn left past the garage."*
Prompt	7/9a	37	Reminder of what you want to say. *"I am going to use my notes as a prompt, rather than reading from them."*
Proposition	7/9a	36	A statement which is to be discussed. *"My group put forward the proposition that 'school uniform should be abolished."*
Proposer	8/9	69	The person who puts forward the proposition. *"I am going to be the proposer for our group and put forward our statement."*
Purpose	7/8b	32	What the author or speaker intended. *"My purpose in writing you this note in this way is to make sure you are absolutely clear about what you need to do."*
Register	7/4	17	Way of speaking. *"I spoke using a formal register, when I was playing the part of the teacher telling someone off."*

Word	Unit	Page	Definition and example
Research activity	7/8a	30	Exploring and looking things up. "Our group, as part of a research activity on earthquakes, went to the library to look in the Geography section and use the Internet."
Response	9/3	80	An answer to something that has been said. "My response to the ideas put forward was to agree with them."
Role	7/5	19	A part that is played. "You take on the role of the student and I'll play the role of the teacher."
Second	9/3	79	To put an argument in favour or against a motion in a debate.
Speaking and listening context	7/5	19	A situation where you will be involved in talking and listening to others talk. "The speaking and listening context here is that you are telling a friend a secret and asking her not to tell anyone else."
Spidergram	7/8b	34	A diagram which connects information by drawing lines between different points, like a spider's web.
Stereotype	7/4	16	Unoriginal, predictable character. "The description of the deaf granny with a stick was stereotypical; my gran wears jeans and trainers!"
Structure	7/5	18	Way of organising what is being said or written. "I used a logical structure, rather than a disorganised one, in what I was saying."
Tone	8/1	44	The way in which you express what you have to say. "I used a persuasive tone, in order to make my point convincingly."
Verbal	8/2	48	Spoken. "I gave a verbal account of what I saw."
Volume	7/1	6	Loudness or softness. "I increased the volume of my voice, because I wanted the whole class to be able to hear me."
Vocabulary	7/4	17	Choice of words. "I think I need to broaden my vocabulary; I don't use a wide enough range of words."
Working in role	9/7	89	To act the part of a different character from your own, while carrying out an activity or discussion. "Working in roles they had been given beforehand, they acted out the situation."

Further resources

Most useful resources will come from the media, mainly television and radio, and can demonstrate different ways of speaking for different purposes and show how active listening can be very important.

It is possible to tape current programmes from the BBC which give models of speaking and which can stimulate classroom ideas for speaking games. The following is a list of programmes that have been used in classrooms.

Check the weekly 6.30pm slot on BBC Radio 4 where there are often panel games, reviews and situation comedies. They provide aural activities that can be a lot of fun. There are also radio dramas available on Radios 3 and 4 which provide useful listening resources as well as material to discuss.

Radio

The following are all on BBC Radio 4

Just a minute

A speaking and listening game where contestants have to speak for a minute on a given subject without hesitation, repetition or deviation. Points are given to "challenges" and promote listening because contestants have to spot when the rules are broken by the speakers.

Call my bluff

This is also broadcast on television. Teams are given obscure words and have to give definitions with only one member of the team giving the right one. This can be very funny and focuses on how convincing a speaker can be. The listening team have to decide which is the accurate definition.

Today

This is a morning news programme and offers a range of speaking registers. Some of the political interviews are very useful in discussing how incisive questioning and careful listening operate, especially when politicians do not want to answer the questions.

The Now show

This is a satirical comedy review that offers a range of language uses, mainly for comedy, but provide good models of how language can be changed and used effectively.

Desert island discs

Although you may not wish to listen to all of this, it is a good model of how to produce a "mini biography" from a "celebrity" through their selection of music. This can be undertaken with books as well.

There are also excellent programmes that review books and films and discuss the media. These differ as the schedules change and your teacher should be able to spot them quite easily.

Television programmes

Stand-up comedy

This is obviously a good resource to demonstrate how language can work to create humour! As schedules change, your teacher will be able to identify appropriate comedians and some are available on video. Although there are many good examples, the following comedians are particularly good at "telling stories" and careful listening will spot how they link their jokes and ideas to form a "shaggy dog story".

- Victoria Wood ● Ben Elton ● Jasper Carrott

Situation comedies

Careful watching of situation comedies will show how characters are formed through language use and interchange. They can also be useful material in discussing how oral speech works in creating humour, pathos and many operate at different levels. The following have been used in classrooms effectively:

- Only fools and horses ● Our family
- The vicar of Dibley ● Keeping up appearances
- 2.4 children ● Blackadder

Reviews

These are normally a collection of sketches and are useful examples of how language works to create stereotypes and characters as well as providing good material for discussion on audiences.

- Goodness gracious me ● Harry Enfield and chums
- The fast show

are all examples of these types of programmes.

Chat Shows

The chat show has become one of the most popular genres on television and can be found on all channels. These can be very useful in discussing how interviews are conducted and how people present themselves as personalities through their use of language. They can also be used as models for classroom activities. Your teacher will check which are appropriate and available at the time but it would be interesting to compare Michael Parkinson with Ali G to see how interview technique works to achieve the programme's purpose.

Tapes

There is quite a lot of taped material that can be used for listening purposes and most of them can be obtained through the BBC Publications office. The following have been used effectively:

Great Speeches

This is a two-tape collection of speeches from the whole of the twentieth century. They include the very famous ones of Martin Luther King and Winston Churchill but also less well known speeches that show the effect of rhetoric. There is a book of transcriptions available so that students can study the actual words.

Talking Heads 1 and 2

These are tapes of Alan Bennett's monologues and can be studied to show the use of spoken language from a range of characters, situations, times and has proved a good resource for discussion of irony. The BBC publish both texts.

Under Milk Wood

Dylan Thomas' work is available on tape and is a good example of how spoken language can be literary and lyrical. Extracts from this can be discussed and used as examples for streams of consciousness.